Religion Matters: On the Significance of Religion in Global Issues

Edited by:
Christine Schliesser, Zurich University, Switzerland
S. Ayse Kadayifci-Orellana, Georgetown University, USA
Pauline Kollontai, York St. John University, UK

Policy makers, academics and practitioners worldwide are increasingly paying attention to the role of religion in global issues. This development is clearly noticeable in conflict resolution, development or climate change, to name just a few pressing issues of global relevance. Up to now, no book series has yet attempted to analyze the role of religion in current global issues in a coherent and systematic way that pertains to academics, policy makers and practitioners alike. The Sustainable Development Goals (SDGs) serve as a dynamic frame of reference. "Religion Matters" provides cutting edge scholarship in a concise format and accessible language, thereby addressing academics, practitioners and policy makers.

On the Significance of Religion in Conflict and Conflict Resolution
Christine Schliesser, S. Ayse Kadayifci-Orellana and Pauline Kollontai

On the Significance of Religion for Global Diplomacy
Philip McDonagh, Kishan Manocha, John Neary, and Lucia Vázquez Mendoza

On the Significance of Religion in Violence Against Women and Girls
Elisabet le Roux and Sandra Iman Pertek

For more information about this series, please visit: https://www.routledge.com/religion/series/RELMAT

"Innovative, evidence-based and thought-provoking. The authors analyse, critique and chart a way forward for both faith-inspired and secular actors working on some of the most pertinent issues of our times. This book is not only a must-read, but a roadmap for women's dignity."

Azza Karam, *Secretary General,*
Religions for Peace

"Through an analytical exploration based on stories of agency and wisdom of Christian and Muslim women and religious leaders, this authoritative and insightful book proposes an unmatched view of religion and the imperative to consider the positive role faith can play in ending VAWG."

Angelica Pino, *Grants Manager, SVRI*

"This is a nuanced and accessible analysis of the significance of religion in VAWG in two faith traditions, Christianity and Islam. Its focus on women's religious experiences in the context of violence fills a gap in the literature available for academics, policymakers and practitioners."

Brenda Bartelink, *University of Groningen,*
The Netherlands

"When working with gender equality in religious societies, I often felt overwhelmed and confused. Having read this book, I feel much better equipped to navigate the complexity. It is clear, pedagogical and full of real voices. I warmly recommend to all."

Virginia Manzitti, *Head of Sector, European*
Commission DEVCO/INTPA

"A must-read for all practitioners, academics and policymakers committed to ending violence against women and girls. Without shying away from the complexity, le Roux and Pertek state the case and offer essential recommendations for secular and religious actors to more effectively collaborate to end violence."

Andrea Kaufmann, *World Vision International*

"This book is for those who want a more nuanced understanding of the ambiguous role of religion in VAWG, based on the authors' own research experience and the projects of various organizations. You will enjoy the differentiated approach based on sound, up-to-date research."

Benjamin Kalkum, *Development Worker for GIZ Zambia*

ON THE SIGNIFICANCE OF RELIGION IN VIOLENCE AGAINST WOMEN AND GIRLS

In this ground-breaking volume, the authors explore two sides of religion: the ways in which it contributes to violence against women and girls (VAWG) and the ways it counters it. Recognising the very real impact of religion on the lives of women and girls, it prioritises experiences and learnings from empirical research and of practitioners, and their activities at grassroots-level, to better understand the nature and root causes of VAWG. Drawing on research done in Christian and Muslim communities in various fragile settings with high religiosity, this book avoids simplistically assigning blame to any one religion, instead engaging with the commonalities of how religion and religious actors influence norms and behaviours that impact VAWG. If the sustainable development goal of ending all forms of VAWG is to be achieved, how should actors in the international development sector engage with religion and religious actors? This book unpacks the nature of religion and religious actors in relation to VAWG, with the aim of giving greater clarity on how to (and how not to) engage with this crucial issue.

Combining cutting-edge research with case studies and pragmatic recommendations for academics, policymakers and practitioners, this concise and easily accessible volume helps instigate discussion and engagement with the incredibly important relationships between religion and VAWG.

Elisabet le Roux is Research Director of the Unit for Religion and Development Research at Stellenbosch University, South Africa.

Sandra Iman Pertek is Postdoctoral Fellow at the University of Birmingham, UK, and gender specialist in humanitarian, development and forced displacement settings.

ON THE SIGNIFICANCE OF RELIGION IN VIOLENCE AGAINST WOMEN AND GIRLS

Elisabet le Roux and Sandra Iman Pertek

Routledge
Taylor & Francis Group

LONDON AND NEW YORK

Designed cover image: Regina Baumhauer, Open Letter
9–11, 2003, oil, screen print on canvas, 153 cm x 175 cm

First published 2023
by Routledge
4 Park Square, Milton Park, Abingdon, Oxon OX14 4RN

and by Routledge
605 Third Avenue, New York, NY 10158

Routledge is an imprint of the Taylor & Francis Group, an informa business

British Library Cataloguing-in-Publication Data
A catalogue record for this book is available from the British Library

ISBN: 978-0-367-76950-5 (hbk)
ISBN: 978-0-367-76949-9 (pbk)
ISBN: 978-1-003-16908-6 (ebk)

DOI: 10.4324/9781003169086

Typeset in Bembo
by codeMantra

CONTENTS

AUTHORS

Dr Elisabet le Roux is Research Director of the Unit for Religion and Development Research at Stellenbosch University, South Africa. To date, she has delivered a range of evaluation and formative research projects in 24 countries across four continents, with a particular focus on violence against women and girls, gender equality, women's participation and a critical lens on the important roles of religion and culture. She has done this research with and for intergovernmental agencies, government departments, development networks, faith-based organisations, non-governmental organisations and research networks. She has significant experience in managing consortium-led projects which have a sector-wide learning agenda, and the majority of her research to date has been done in conflict-affected communities. Elisabet has a proven track record in mixed methodology research including a series of longer-term, multi-country evaluations and studies. More recently, she has been prioritising the development and use of innovative, creative, participatory and feminist research methods, and she is increasingly assisting development organisations in developing their overarching strategic approaches to religion, culture and violence against women and girls.

Dr Sandra Iman Pertek is Postdoctoral Fellow at the University of Birmingham, School of Social Policy and Gender and Social Development Specialist with expertise in faith and violence against women and girls (VAWG) with over a decade's experience in humanitarian, development and migration settings. She is an inter-disciplinary and mixed-methods researcher with a track record of programmatic and research leadership, policy influence and capacity building. Her research integrates an intersectional and ecological analysis to explore the intersection of gender-based violence and religion in forced migration. She led a number of research assignments, including in Ethiopia, Jordan, Poland, Tunisia, Turkey, UK, Ukraine and Zambia, and remotely across regions. As Senior Policy Advisor on Gender, she authored Gender Justice Policy of Islamic Relief Worldwide and spearheaded a gender integration strategy in its global operations, by building staff capacities, institutional partnerships and piloting faith-sensitive VAWG programmes. As consultant she worked with and for governmental, inter- and non-governmental organisations, including for the Home Office UK, GIZ and Islamic Development Bank, and contributed to a range of women's organisations. She has recently coordinated several multi-stakeholder initiatives to strengthen protection from VAWG in forced displacement, including the integration of religion and faith actors into protection frameworks.

ACKNOWLEDGEMENTS

As authors of this volume, we would like to thank all of the participants that took part in our studies. Thank you so much for your willingness to speak with us and share your thoughts and experiences. This book would clearly not have been possible without you. Also special thanks to all of the interpreters and transcribers who helped us in the various countries we worked.

Thank you to all of the organisations that invited us to do research with and for them. It has been a great privilege to learn from you about working at the intersection of religion and VAWG.

Thank you to the editors of the series, Christine Schliesser, S. Ayse Kadayifci-Orellana and Pauline Kollontai, for inviting us to write this book. A special thanks to Christine Schliesser for all her support throughout.

Finally, thank you to the Institute of Social Ethics of Zurich University, particularly to Prof. Dr Michael Coors, and to the Open Access Publication Fund for the Humanities and Social Sciences of Zurich University, who supported us with open access Fees, as well Birmingham Global at University of Birmingham who supported us with indexing fees.

Elisabet le Roux would like to thank my co-author, Sandra Iman Pertek, for writing this book with me. It has been a joy to work with you and I have learnt so much in the process! I also thank my family for their support. A final big thank you to all of the people I've worked with over the years, who have challenged, influenced and moulded my thinking in countless ways.

Sandra Iman Pertek would like to thank the University of Birmingham for hosting and funding my doctoral research as part of the School of Social Policy Studentship, and Jenny Phillimore and Lisa Goodson for supporting my doctoral/post-doctoral journey. I am grateful to the co-author of this book – Elisabet le Roux – for collaboration on this manuscript, patience and valuable comments. Finally, I wish to thank my family who supported me along the way.

ABBREVIATIONS

AWET	Apostolic Women Empowerment Trust
CAR	Central African Republic
CoH	Channels of Hope
DRC	Democratic Republic of Congo
DG	DEVCO European Commission Directorate-General for International Cooperation and Development
FBO	Faith-based organisation
FGD	Focus group discussion
FGM/C	Female genital mutilation and/or cutting
EU	European Union
GBV	Gender-based violence
INGO	International non-governmental organisation
IDPs	Internally displaced persons
IRE	Islamic Relief Ethiopia
IRW	Islamic Relief Worldwide
KII	Key informant interview
MUZ	Anglican Mothers' Union in Zambia
NGO	Non-governmental organisation
PBUH	Peace be upon him
SDG	Sustainable Development Goal
UN	United Nations
UN	Trust Fund UN Trust Fund to End Violence against Women
VAWG	Violence against women and girls

EXECUTIVE SUMMARY

Globally, violence against women and girls (VAWG) remains a pervasive and urgent public health, human rights and development issue. In this third volume of the series "Religion Matters – On the Significance of Religion in Global Issues", the authors explore the complex role of religion in VAWG, focusing on Sustainable Development Goal 5: "Achieve gender equality and empower all women and girls".

The interest in the role of religion and religious actors in various development issues increased considerably in the last two decades, including concerning the role of religion and religious actors in gender equality and non-violence. This book expands understanding of how religion affects the lives and safety of women and girls. Based on the empirical and in-depth exploratory research conducted in several countries across regions and within different Christian and Islamic contexts with high religiosity and fragility, the authors identify and unpack the ways in which religion and religious actors contribute to VAWG, but also play a role in addressing VAWG and its consequences.

The volume unites the perspectives of two different faith traditions (Christianity and Islam) in an analytical and practical exploration of how religion matters in the protection and vulnerability of women and girls to gendered violence. Using Ter Haar's four main categories of religious resources – religious ideas, religious practices, religious organisation and religious experiences – as a conceptual framework for organising the discussions in the empirical chapters, the authors uncover a range of functions and impacts of religious resources in influencing experiences of VAWG, combining theoretical and practical reflection for research, policy and practice.

In reflecting on how religion contributes to VAWG, Le Roux's critical analyses from a Christian perspective show that religion can contribute to vulnerability to VAWG and victimisation, in the intersection between religion and culture, the vilification of sex and sexuality, the entanglement of religion and patriarchy, and where religious experiences challenge accepted VAWG prevention practice. Pertek's critical analyses from a Muslim perspective indicate how religion can be an intersecting risk factor with religious ideas shaping ambiguous interpretations and attitudes to violence and with religious practices silencing victims and causing in/direct harm. She also explores religious experience, endurance and spiritual violence, and where religious organisation may dictate patriarchal (dis)order.

In reflecting on how religion can counter VAWG, the authors' findings reveal that religion, religious leaders and religious communities often contribute to VAWG prevention and response. Le Roux's discussion of Christian settings highlights the great potential of drawing on the authority of the Bible, leveraging religious leadership, recognising the transformative power of prayer and understanding and responding to context. Pertek's findings from Muslim contexts emphasise the value of religious beliefs in meaning-making and building resistance; religious practices, such as praying and reading the Qur'an, in strengthening coping mechanisms and the role of religious experiences in empowering and healing survivors of VAWG. She also points to the importance of mobilising policy in religious organisations for faith-inspired anti-VAWG practice.

Drawing on the empirical chapters and accompanying joint reflections, the authors offer researchers, practitioners and policymakers pragmatic guidance on moving forward in their engagement with religion on VAWG prevention and response. Seven key implications from the preceding chapters' discussions are identified, which, in turn, can serve as guidance or priorities for these different stakeholders: (1) engage religious resources and religious actors on VAWG; (2) recognise the role and potential of religious experience; (3) recognise the agency of religious women survivors; (4) engage with religion when working with perpetrators who are religious; (5) prioritise religious literacy; (6) use a hybrid and pragmatic understanding of religion and (7) strengthen collaboration between secular and religious actors.

PART I

Introduction

1

WHY RELIGION MATTERS IN VIOLENCE AGAINST WOMEN AND GIRLS

Elisabet le Roux and Sandra Iman Pertek

Introduction

Violence against women and girls (VAWG) is internationally recognised as a significant public health, human rights and development issue. Even though almost three decades have passed since the 1993 UN Declaration on the Elimination of Violence against Women and the 1995 Beijing Platform for Action, accompanied by various global and regional efforts to address the issue, VAWG remains as pervasive globally. In 2021, WHO published the first global systematic review of scientific data on the prevalence of intimate-partner violence and non-partner sexual violence. Relying on data from surveys and studies conducted globally between 2000 and 2018, the study found that 31% of women and girls aged 15–49 years, and 30% of women and girls aged 15 years and older, have experienced physical and/or sexual violence from a current or former intimate partner and/or sexual violence from a non-partner (WHO, 2021). The data shows "unequivocally that violence against women is pervasive globally. It is not a small problem that only occurs in some pockets of society; rather, it is a global public health

DOI: 10.4324/9781003169086-2

problem of pandemic proportions, affecting hundreds of millions of women and requiring urgent action" (WHO, 2021:xix).

Within international development, religion was until recently side-lined or ignored. However, since the 2000s, interest in the role of religion and religious actors in various development issues increased considerably (Deneulin and Rakodi, 2011; Jones and Petersen, 2011; Swart and Nell, 2016). Part of this shift includes recognising the role of religion and religious actors in gender equality and non-violence. Especially global, institutional acknowledgement of the role of religion and religious actors in addressing gender inequality and VAWG has become more common over the last decade, as evidenced by the statements, publications, actions and funding decisions of key intergovernmental agencies within international development. For example:

- a global Platform on 'Gender Equality and Religion' was launched in 2017 by UN Women, the UN Population Fund, UK Department for International Development (now renamed the Foreign, Commonwealth & Development Office) and the International Partnership on Religion and Sustainable Development;
- in 2018, the Gender Equality, Human Rights and Democratic Governance of the Directorate-General for International Cooperation and Development (DG DEVCO) at the European Commission, with the support of the Methodological and Knowledge Sharing Support Programme, launched the Agora on Religion and Development as a safe learning space for DG DEVCO and other European Union (EU) staff working on religion and/or external action to progress in their understanding of the nexus between religion and development and included sessions specifically on religion and gender;
- the EU's Gender Action Plan III (launched in 2020) stipulates that the EU should support the mobilisation of religious actors for gender equality;
- a recent brief published by the UN Trust Fund to End Violence against Women (UN Trust Fund) showcases the work done

by religious actors, and the lessons learned on working with religious actors, on VAWG prevention in a range of projects funded globally by the UN Trust Fund (Le Roux and Palm, 2021);

• the Spotlight Initiative, a global multi-year partnership between the EU and UN to eliminate all forms of VAWG by 2030, has supported various initiatives globally that work with religious actors to address VAWG and/or promote gender equality.

With VAWG recognised as a major development issue, and global acknowledgement of the role of religion and religious actors in development, it is arguably obvious that engaging with religion and religious actors on VAWG should form part of holistic VAWG prevention and response. Yet, it appears that many within the international development community remain hesitant to engage with religion and religious actors, especially on VAWG (Le Roux, 2015; Ager and Ager, 2016; Olivier, 2016; Le Roux and Loots, 2017; Khalaf-Elledge, 2020; Khalaf-Elledge, 2021).

As our research and experiences indicate that this hesitancy is at least partly due to misunderstanding or incomplete understanding of religion and the role that it plays in VAWG, this book strives to contribute to a better understanding of the role of religion in relation to VAWG. It explores both the ways in which religion contributes to VAWG and the ways it counters it. In doing so, we engage with empirical research we (individually) conducted in several countries and contexts with high religiosity and fragility. By exploring these different settings, we aim to identify and unpack the ways in which religion, religious leaders and religious communities contribute to VAWG prevention and response as well as how they contribute to its continued perpetration. While exploring these issues, we are guided by a need not only for thorough analysis but also for practical applicability. In other words, we intertwine the empirical exploration with theoretical reflection in relation to what it means to practitioners and policymakers in their (potential) engagement with religion and religious actors on VAWG.

Background to the volume

This book is the third volume in the series "Religion Matters – On the Significance of Religion in Global Issues". The overarching theme of the series explores the significance of religion in global issues, with each volume focusing directly or indirectly on a specific Sustainable Development Goal (SDG). With this book, we focus on religion and VAWG. This relates to Sustainable Goal #5 ("Achieve gender equality and empower all women and girls") and specifically its second target, namely to "eliminate all forms of violence against all women and girls in the public and private spheres, including trafficking and sexual and other types of exploitation" (UN, n.d., unpaginated). Aside from SDG 5, this volume also connects with other SDGs, including SDG 16 ("Promote peaceful and inclusive societies for sustainable development, provide access to justice for all and build effective, accountable and inclusive institutions at all levels") and SDG 17 ("Strengthen the means of implementation and revitalise the global partnership for sustainable development").

Being aware of the real-life impact religious beliefs have on the lives and safety of women and girls, this volume prioritises experiences and learnings from empirical research and of practitioners and their activities at grassroots level to better understand the nature and impact of religion on VAWG. We account for the double-edged nature of religion: the role it plays in driving, but also in countering, the violence that women and girls experience daily. The book unites the perspectives of two different religious traditions (Christianity and Islam) in an analytical and practical exploration of how religion matters in both the protection *and* vulnerability of women and girls.

Through its in-depth exploration of both Islamic and Christian settings, the volume contributes to a richer, more nuanced understanding of the role of religion in VAWG. In turn, we develop general guidelines for engagement with and on religion around VAWG, thereby underlining its relevance beyond only the academic sphere into the realms of policymaking and praxis.

The authors of this volume have extensive experience – as practitioners and as researchers – in VAWG prevention and response praxis. Elisabet le Roux draws on the findings from a range of research projects she was part of over the last 12 years in various countries including, but not limited to, the Democratic Republic of Congo, Rwanda, Liberia, Uganda, Burundi, Zambia, South Africa and Colombia (multi-country studies where in-country fieldwork was not conducted are not included in this list). Sandra Pertek relies on her PhD research with forced migrant women in Turkey and Tunisia as well as a decade's experience of working on gender, VAWG and religion integration in international development. As stated earlier, the different settings explored in this volume all have high levels of religiosity and fragility.

This book is a short volume, written in an easily readable, accessible way. The hope is that it can serve as an entry point for researchers, practitioners and policymakers to better understand the intersection between religion and VAWG. As such, it aims to form part of a nuanced discussion that avoids being religious advocacy or simplistic condemnation of religion, offering a balanced account of the religion and VAWG nexus.

Understanding violence against women and girls

In this book, we use the term 'violence against women and girls' (VAWG), rather than gender-based violence (GBV) or sexual- and gender-based violence (SGBV). All three of these terms are used within the international development sphere, fairly interchangeably, to denote the violence that women and girls experience. The term GBV appears to be the most commonly used, yet we intentionally do not use this term. The term 'GBV' originates from within the women's rights movement, where it was used to indicate that women's exposure to violence is due to patriarchy and that the myriad forms of violence women and girls experience is a result of gender inequality. Using the term 'GBV' was part of the political agenda of feminism, emphasising the structural drivers of the violence women and girls are exposed to and the need for gender equality (COFEM, 2017). However, calls for gender neutrality and gender sensitivity have led to the term 'GBV' no longer being used to refer only to the violences that women and girls experience but also to all violences suffered by anyone based on their gender or gender identity. This shift in definition has been embraced by influential governments, policymakers and funders. For example, the US government officially sees GBV as targeting both men and women, defining it as "...directed at an individual based on his or her biological sex, gender identity, or perceived adherence to socially defined norms of masculinity and femininity..." (USAID, n.d., unpaginated). The EU's definition of GBV uses gender only as a demographic indicator, defining it as "...violence directed against a person because of that person's gender or as violence that affects persons of a particular gender disproportionately" – although it does state that women and girls are most affected by GBV (European Commission, n.d).

We choose to use the term 'violence against women and girls' to avoid any confusion and emphasise that we are focusing on the role that religion plays in violences that *women and girls* experience. As such, we draw on the definition of VAWG as captured in the UN Declaration on the Elimination of Violence against Women:

> any act of gender-based violence that results in, or is likely to result in, physical, sexual or psychological harm or suffering to women [and girls], including threats of such acts, coercion or arbitrary deprivation of liberty, whether occurring in public or in private life.
>
> *(OHCHR, n.d., addition by authors)*

We also recognise that combining 'women' and 'girls' in a definition runs the risk of ignoring or marginalising the specific and unique forms of violence that girls (and not women) experience. We nevertheless still choose to engage with both (as violence against women *and* girls), as the violences that women experience and the violences that girls experience have many drivers in common. We therefore choose to include girls in our focus, as we believe it is important to emphasise that women experience violence across their life cycle and not only when they reach adulthood.

We also wish to emphasise that women and girls do not only experience violence simply because of being women or girls but also based on their intersecting identities. Intersectionality empha-sises that women are oppressed and become vulnerable by inter-locking systems of oppression, such as sexism, racism and ageism (Crenshaw, 1991, Collins, 2015; Armstrong et al., 2018; Kumar, 2018), and across different levels of socio-ecology (Heise, 1998; Pertek, 2022). Women's risk of experiencing violence is due to power imbalances and social inequalities associated with differ-ent identity categories (e.g. race, gender and class) and wider cir-cumstances (e.g. occupation and location). This means that not all women's level of risk of experiencing VAWG is the same nor are their needs the same in the aftermath of experiencing VAWG (Crenshaw, 1991; Palm and Le Roux, 2021). Furthermore, women and girls experience a spectrum of violence over time and place, with the real-life boundaries between different acts of violence being indefinite and messy (Gray, 2019; Pertek, 2022). Our gen-eral discussion of VAWG in this volume does not mean to ignore this reality, but it is beyond the scope of this book to go into inter-sectionality in more depth.

Understanding religion

In studying religion, some approaches study religion from within (e.g. religious studies), while other approaches attempt to under-stand the nature of religion as a social and cultural phenomenon (e.g. social sciences) (Rakodi, 2007). In this book, we follow the second approach. We are not concerned with the truth claims of Christianity and Islam (the two specific religions studied in this volume), but rather focus on understanding how these religions impact drivers of and resistance to VAWG.

There is no universal definition of religion. Within social sciences, there is a tendency to distinguish between substantive and functional definitions of religion. Substantive definitions focus on what religion *is*, paying attention to the cross-cultural attri-butes of religion that differentiates it from other social phenomena and emphasising belief in a transcendental reality (Rakodi, 2007). Functional definitions, on the other hand, focus on what religion *does*. These definitions emphasise the instrumental role religion plays in constructing people's worldviews and establishing social cohesion (Rakodi, 2007; Schilbrack, 2013).

Both substantive and functional definitions of religion face criticism. Amongst other things, substantive definitions are criticised for excluding certain religions. For example, when a specific substantive definition is based on theism (a belief in an eternal God Creator), it will not include Buddhism as a religion. Functional definitions are accused of being too inclusive, as these definitions make it "virtually impossible to set any substantive boundary to religion and, thus, to distinguish it from other socio-cultural phenomena" (Spiro, 1966:89). Considering these criticisms, we chose to follow a hybrid definition that includes both functional and substantial elements. We understand religion as offering a normative order linked to a set of practices (functional) *and* belief in theistic or nontheistic realities (substantive): "The key is that the rituals and the ethics of the activity need to connect the practitioners to a super-empirical reality" (Schilbrack, 2013:316–317). With such a definition, nontheistic traditions can be recognised as religious, without all forms of communal meaning-making also being included as 'religious' (Schilbrack, 2013).

In addition to the hybrid definition guiding this book, we recognise that religion carries different meanings for different people. Having conducted research within various communities across the globe, we realise the importance of acknowledging how those in the communities we work with understand religion (Schliesser et al., 2021). Therefore, we also rely on a pragmatic definition based on subjective meanings linked to an individual's experiences with religion. We consider hybrid and pragmatic definitions of religion complementary and helpful in deconstructing and understanding religion's roles in VAWG experiences.

In conceptualising religion in VAWG, we attend to multiple religious resources, helping us operationalise religious influences on human experiences. Gerrie ter Haar highlights that religious resources, like all human resources, can be used for political and development purposes (Ter Haar, 2005). Such reflection is important for this book, which strives to discuss not only how religion can drive VAWG but also how it can oppose VAWG. Through defining and unpacking four different kinds of religious resources, Ter Haar focuses attention on the potential of religion and religious communities to contribute to the common good:

> The most important reason for paying serious attention to the religious dimension of people's lives is the need to make maximum use of whatever resources exist for development purposes. Given that religion is an integral part of the lives of millions of people, it can be considered a human resource of significant importance. Since it is widely accepted in policy circles that development, if it is to be effective and lasting, should build on people's own resources, it make sense to include their religious or spiritual resources and not material and intellectual ones only.
>
> *(Ter Haar, 2011:8)*

Ter Haar's conceptualisation of religious resources is practical, lending itself to pragmatic use in our volume. We have selected to use Ter Haar's four main categories of religious resources as a framework for organising the discussions in the empirical chapters (Chapters 2,3,7 and 8). She differentiates between four main elements of religion, which correspond to four main categories that can be found in all the world's religious traditions, namely religious ideas, religious practices, religious organisation and religious experiences:

- *Religious ideas* refer to the content of belief, and exploring this resource seeks to understand what people actually believe and why;
- *Religious practices* refer to the way people act and behave on the basis of their belief, often in the form of ritual behaviour;
- *Religious organisation* refers to the community component of religion, that is, how people organise themselves on the basis of their belief;
- *Religious experience* refers to the psychic attitudes and experiences that religion may incite in believers, for example, the subjective experience of inner transformation (Ter Haar, 2011).

Other conceptualisations of religion also exist. For example, Frazer and Friedli (2015) identify five ways of thinking about religion, namely understanding religion as community, as a set of teachings, as spirituality, as practice and as discourse. They related these components with the analysis of dividers and connectors in conflict resolution. Woodhead (2011) combines concepts of religion according to the character of specific study design and suggests a taxonomy of five concepts to enable the study of religion: culture, identity, relationship, practice and power.

However, we selected Ter Haar's conceptualisation of religious resources as we consider it a more useful framework, compared to other conceptualisations, for our discussion of religion and VAWG. First, the Ter Haar framework offers four broad categories that correspond to different areas of human life: religious ideas (cognition), practices (behaviour), organisation (community) and experience (emotional/spiritual). These matter in VAWG and VAWG research, and thus the framework can serve as a heuristic tool for mapping religious influences on VAWG in a structured way. Second, the focus on resources allows for exploring both the substantive and functional components of religion. In other words, both what a religion *is* and what it *does* can be explored under this framework of 'resources'. Third, as this book aims to contribute to the conversation on how religion can support efforts to end VAWG, a discussion focused on resources allows recognition of the potential positive contributions of religion and religious actors without instrumentalising them. At the same time, we also recognise that religious resources are not necessarily positive – as is explored in more detail in Chapters 3 and 4. Fourth, a focus on resources allows for a comparative discussion of religions that continue to recognise the uniqueness of each religious tradition and the setting in which it is practised. As such, the religious resources framework serves as the overarching structure for all four empirical chapters contained in this book, illustrating the potentials and pitfalls of religion in VAWG.

A final note on terminology is needed. In this volume we use the term 'religious actors' as a general term that includes faith-based organisations, religious networks, church-based agencies, religious groups, religious associations and charities, interfaith networks and councils, missionary organisations, religious community organisations and religious leaders (Le Roux, 2021).

Interpretivist approach

In writing this book, we followed an interpretivist approach. Interpretivist approaches are based on the belief that reality is socially constructed and made meaningful through people's understanding and interpretations of events (Putnam and Banghart, 2017). As people's knowledge of reality is deemed a social construction, interpretivist approaches stand in marked contrast to positivist approaches that claim objective knowledge (Chowdhury, 2014).

An interpretivist approach was deemed appropriate for this book as it allows the researcher to search for the meanings and motives behind people's actions (Chowdhury, 2014). Such an approach is needed when it is not fully understood why certain events occur, or how these events are being dealt with and understood (Bryman, 2008; Babbie and Mouton, 2010). An interpretivist approach thus allows us to focus on lived experience, which is needed because of the pragmatic and hybrid definition of religion that the book embraces. The hybrid definition of religion recognises both the functional and substantive elements of religion, while the pragmatic definition recognises the subjective meanings linked to an individual's experiences with religion. An interpretivist approach, acknowledging that meaning-making is subjective experience, is therefore appropriate for this book's understanding of religion. Additionally, interpretivist approaches value and promote qualitative data, recognising its importance for understanding the uniqueness of a particular situation (Chowdhury, 2014). As all of the empirical studies that this book relies on are qualitative, this again points to the appropriateness of following an interpretivist approach. For data analysis, both authors deployed inductive, systematic thematic analysis, as a flexible method of qualitative analysis which fits well within an interpretivist paradigm.

Pertek, in analysing the data from her doctoral study (which forms a core part of Chapters 4 and 8), followed a specific form of interpretivist approach, namely social constructivism (Schwandt, 1998). In her study, she paid attention to the subjective expressions of religious ideas and practices in their socio-cultural contexts. In her chapters, therefore, Pertek refers to the way that the social world, and so in part the religious world, was seen by respondents and how they understood their experiences (Denzin and Lincoln, 1998). In doing so, she captured how respondents constructed meaning and knowledge of their own lived experiences of religion and VAWG.

Bringing together academics, practitioners and policymakers

Ending VAWG will require partnership and collaboration across different sectors of society: "Unprecedented worldwide public, professional and political interest currently offers exceptional opportunities for action. Strong leadership and coordination, to guide a multisector response and ensure coherence across sectors, can and must be mobilised" (García-Moreno and Temmerman, 2015:187). This volume strives to contribute to such collaboration by engaging with and exploring learning on religion and VAWG in a way that is relevant to academics, policymakers and practitioners and can facilitate conversation between these groups by highlighting areas of joint interest and potential synergies. In doing so, we offer concrete recommendations for each group to enable better understanding and collaboration.

We also aim to contribute to crossing the divide that still exists between the so-called secular and religious sectors within international development, with mistrust marring collaboration in addressing VAWG (Le Roux and Loots, 2017; Khalaf-Elledge, 2020). Improved mutual understanding and trust appears to be much needed in order for multisectoral collaboration to flourish. For example, in a 2015 scoping study on the role of religious communities in VAWG prevention and response (Le Roux, 2015), the key informants from different faith-based international organisations described the international development arena as thoroughly secular and prejudiced against them: "(A)ll of the participants felt that the knee-jerk reaction of their secular counterparts was still to distrust and avoid faith actors" (Le Roux and Loots, 2017:738). Similarly, research on faith inclusion in VAWG prevention with humanitarian service providers identified that same distrust and adverse attitudes towards engagement with religious actors, as captured in this statement by a Head of Mission from an international non-governmental organisation (NGO):

> Most of the arguments against what you should be doing against providing a service would be coming from a religious standpoint. So I would see more as a challenge, religion as a whole, more as a challenge and not as an asset in my work…
>
> *(Head of Mission from international NGO,*
> *interview by Pertek, 2019)*

This attitude is echoed in a study conducted between 2015 and 2019 (Khalaf-Elledge, 2020) studying different levels of development practitioners (government aid agencies, recipient organisations and local women's rights activists). The study found that:

> an outdated, normative, and binary understanding of secularity's neutrality and religion's irrationality has rendered Western development organisations significantly religion-blind and skewed their sense of objectivity. A lack of knowledge, interest, and engagement with religion may have fostered an Orientalist mindset that essentialises religion as backwards and subjective.
>
> *(Khalaf-Elledge, 2020:669)*

But secular donors and policymakers argue that it is often challenging to work with religious actors on VAWG. In a small 2021 study with representatives from intergovernmental agencies and government ministries from the Global North, key informants explained the challenges they had in collaborating with religious actors who did not recognise the political and policy regulations and constraints on these agencies and ministries, did not embody the gender principles their programming is supposed to promote and/or were not willing to engage in reflective dialogues on their principles and programming:

But if we find that faith actors are very stubborn, not interested to dialogue, not interested to change or to reflect on theological standpoints, then it's quite hard for us at [our institution] to engage in new partnerships because we have to have this openness for dialogue and the transformational approach. Because then we can trust. But otherwise, I think there will always be this dilemma of mistrust. You know: 'what is really happening in the work we do not see or do not engage with?'

(Informant from government ministry, in Le Roux, 2021)

Through offering honest reflection on and critique of the ways in which religion contributes to VAWG, as well as the ways it counters it, based on empirical studies conducted in various countries and with different religious communities, we hope to advance mutual understanding between actors from different sectors, which can in turn advance partnership and collaboration to end VAWG. The final chapter of the book offers concrete recommendations for academics, practitioners and policymakers, providing pragmatic directions for moving forward in ways that promote collaboration.

Outline of this book

This book unites the perspectives of two different faith traditions (Christianity and Islam) in an analytical and practical exploration of how religion matters in the protection and vulnerability of women and girls to violence. It is an interreligious, interdisciplinary and international exploration, with the aim of being relevant to academics, policymakers and practitioners.

This introductory chapter was preceded by an executive summary. It is followed by the empirical and analytical core of the book, which consists of two main parts (Parts II and III). Part II focuses on how religion drives VAWG. After a brief orientation chapter (Chapter 2), Chapter 3 unpacks the Christian perspective, followed by Chapter 4 exploring the Islamic perspective. This is followed by a joint reflection chapter (Chapter 5), which synthesises, summarises and reflects on the role of religion in driving VAWG *based on the preceding two chapters*.

Part III focuses on how religion counters VAWG. Again, a brief orientation chapter (Chapter 6) will serve as an introduction, followed by le Roux's discussion of the Christian perspective (Chapter 7) and then Pertek's discussion of the Islamic perspective (Chapter 8). Again, a joint reflection chapter follows (Chapter 9), which synthesis, summarises and reflects on the positive role of religion in countering VAWG based on the preceding two chapters.

Part IV contains the final chapter (Chapter 10), which draws together the insights gained from the four empirical chapters and two reflection chapters, framing it as concrete implications and recommendations for research, policy and practice.

References

Ager, A. and Ager, J. (2016). "Sustainable development and religion: Accommodating diversity in a post-secular age", *The Review of Faith & International Affairs*, 14(3): 101–105.

Armstrong, E., Gleckman-Krut, M. and Johnson, L. (2018). "Silence, power, and inequality: An intersectional approach to sexual violence", *Annual Review of Sociology*, 44: 99–122.

Babbie, E. and Mouton, J. (2010). *The practice of social research*. Cape Town: Oxford University Press.

Bryman, A. (2008). *Social research methods*. Oxford: Oxford University Press.

Chowdhury, M.F. (2014). "Interpretivism in aiding our understanding of the contemporary social world", *Open Journal of Philosophy*, 4: 432–438.

COFEM. (2017). *Reframing the language of 'gender-based violence' away from feminist underpinnings*. Feminist Perspectives on Addressing Violence Against Women and Girls Series, Paper No. 2. Viewed from https://cofemsocialchange.org/wp-content/uploads/2018/11/Paper-2-Reframing-language-of-%E2%80%98GBV%E2%80%99-away-from-feminist-underpinnings.pdf [Date accessed: April 6, 2022].

Collins, P.H. (2015). "Intersectionality's definitional dilemmas", *Annual Review of Sociology*, 41: 1–20.

Crenshaw, K. (1991). "Mapping the margins intersectionality, identity politics, and violence against women of colour", *Stanford Law Review*, 43(6): 1241–1299.

Deneulin, S. and Rakodi, C. (2011). "Revisiting religion: Development studies thirty years on", *World Development*, 39(1): 45–54.

Denzin, K. and Lincoln, Y. (1998). *The landscape of qualitative research: Theories and issues*. Thousand Oaks, CA: Sage Publications.

European Commission. (n.d.). *What is gender-based violence?* European Commission. Viewed from https://ec.europa.eu/info/policies/justice-and-fundamental-rights/gender-equality/gender-based-violence/what-gender-based-violence_en [Date accessed: November 17, 2018].

Frazer, O. and Friedli, R. (2015). *Approaching religion in conflict transformation: Concepts, cases and practical implications. Center for Security Studies (CSS) Swiss Federal Institute of Technology*. Zurich: Swiss Federal Institute of Technology (ETH). Viewed from https://css.ethz.ch/content/dam/ethz/special-interest/gess/cis/center-for-securities-studies/pdfs/Approaching-Religion-In-Conflict-Transformation2.pdf [Date accessed: April 12, 2021].

García-Moreno, C. and Temmerman, M. (2015). "Commentary: Actions to end violence against women: A multi-sector approach", *Global Public Health*, 10(2): 186–188.

Gray, H. (2019). "The 'war'/'not-war' divide: Domestic violence in the preventing sexual violence initiative", *The British Journal of Politics and International Relations*, 21(1): 189–206. doi:10.1177/1369148118802470.

Heise, L.L. (1998). "Violence against women: An integrated, ecological framework", *Violence against Women*, 4(3): 262–290.

Jones, B. and Petersen, M.J. (2011). "Instrumental, narrow, normative? Reviewing recent work on religion and development", *Third World Quarterly*, 32(7): 1291–1306.

Khalaf-Elledge, N. (2020). "It's a tricky one" – development practitioners' attitudes towards religion", *Development in Practice*, 30(5): 660–671.

Khalaf-Elledge, N. (2021). *Scoping study: Looking back to look forward. The role of religious actors in gender equality since the Beijing Declaration*. Joint Learning Initiative on Faith and Local Communities. Viewed from https://jliflc.com/resources/scoping-study-looking-back-to-look-forward-the-role-of-religious-actors-in-gender-equality-since-the-beijing-declaration/ [Date accessed: April 6, 2022].

Kumar, C. (2018). "Black feminist intersectional practice working to end violence against women and girls (VAWG)", in S. Nayak and R. Robbins (eds.), *Intersectionality in social work: Activism and practice*. London: Routledge, 150–166.

Le Roux, E. (2015). *A scoping study on the role of faith communities and organisations in prevention and response to sexual and gender-based violence: Implications for policy and practice*. Joint Learning Initiative on

Faith and Local Communities. Viewed from https://jliflc.com/wp-content/uploads/2015/10/Le-Roux_SGBVFaith-scoping-study_REPORT_30Sept15.pdf [Date accessed: March 12, 2019].

Le Roux, E. (2021). *Religion and gender in donor policies and practice. A reflection on government ministry and intergovernmental agency engagement with religious actors in pursuit of SDG 5.* Joint Learning Initiative on Faith and Local Communities. Viewed from https://jliflc.com/wp-content/uploads/2021/11/Layout_LeRoux_Religiongender-in-donor-policiespractice_Final_21Oct21-004.pdf [Date accessed: April 6, 2022].

Le Roux, E. and Loots, L. (2017). "The unhealthy divide: How the secular/faith binary potentially limits GBV prevention and response", *Development in Practice*, 27(5): 733–744.

Le Roux, E. and Palm, S. (2021). *Learning from practice: Engaging faith-based and traditional actors in preventing violence against women and girls.* New York: United Nations Trust Fund to End Violence against Women. Viewed from https://untf.unwomen.org/en/digital-library/publications/2021/07/engaging-faith-based-and-traditional-actors-in-preventing-violence-against-women-and-girls [Date accessed: April 6, 2022].

OHCHR. (n.d.). *Gender-based violence against women and girls.* Viewed from https://www.ohchr.org/en/women/gender-based-violence-against-women-and-girls [Date accessed: April 6, 2022].

Olivier, J. (2016). "Hoist by our own petard: Backing slowly out of religion and development advocacy", *HTS Theological Studies*, 72(4): 1–11.

Palm, S. and Le Roux, E. (2021). *Learning from practice: Exploring intersectional approaches to preventing violence against women and girls.* New York: United Nations Trust Fund to End Violence against Women.

Pertek, S. (2022). "Religion, forced migration and the continuum of violence: An intersectional and ecological analysis". PhD Dissertation, University of Birmingham.

Putnam, L.L. and Banghart, S. (2017). "Interpretative approaches", in C.R. Scott, J.R. Barker, T. Kuhn, J. Keyton, P.K. Turner and L.K. Lewis (eds.), *The International Encyclopedia of Organizational Communication*, 1–17. Wiley Online Library. https://doi.org/10.1002/9781118955567.wbieoc118

Rakodi, C. (2007). *Understanding the roles of religions in development: The approach of the RAD Programme.* Viewed from http://epapers.bham.ac.uk/1494/ [Date accessed: April 6, 2022].

Schilbrack, K. (2013). "What isn't religion?", *The Journal of Religion*, 93(3): 291–218.

Schliesser, C., Kadayifci-Orellana, S.A. and Kollontai, P. (2021). *On the significance of religion in conflict and conflict resolution*. Abindon, Oxon: Routledge.

Schwandt, T. (1998). "Constructivist, interpretivist approaches to human inquiry", in K. Denzin and Y. Lincoln (eds.), *The landscape of qualitative research: Theories and issues*. Thousand Oaks, CA: Sage Publications, 221–259.

Spiro, M. (1966). "Religion: Problems of definition and explanation", in M. Banton (ed.), *Anthropological approaches to the study of religion*. London: Tavistock, 89–90.

Swart, I. and Nell, E. (2016). "Religion and development: The rise of a bibliography", *HTS Teologiese Studies/Theological Studies*, 72(4): a3862.

Ter Haar, G. (2005). "Religion: Source of conflict or resource for peace?", in P. Ostien, J.A. Nasir and F. Kogelmann (eds.), *Comparative perspectives on Shari'ah in Nigeria*. Abuja: Spectrum Books Limited, 303–319.

Ter Haar, G. (2011). "Religion and development: Introducing a new debate", in G. Ter Haar (ed.), *Religion and development: Ways of transforming the world*. London: Hurst and Company, 3–25.

UN. (n.d.). *The 17 goals*. United Nations Department of Economic and Social Affairs: Sustainable Development. Viewed from https://sdgs.un.org/goals [Date accessed: April 6,2022].

USAID. (n.d). *Part 2: GBV definition, prevalence, and global statistics*. Toolkit for Integrating GBV Prevention & Response into Economic Growth Projects. Viewed from https://www.usaid.gov/sites/default/files/documents/1865/USAID%20Toolkit%20GBV%20EG%20Final%20Section%202.pdf [Date accessed: November 27, 2018].

WHO. (2021). *Violence against women prevalence estimates, 2018: Global, regional and national prevalence estimates for intimate partner violence against women and global and regional prevalence estimates for non-partner sexual violence against women*. Viewed from https://www.who.int/publications/i/item/9789240022256 [Date accessed: April 6, 2022].

Woodhead, L. (2011). "Five concepts of religion", *International Review of Sociology*, 21(1): 121–143. doi:10.1080/03906701.2011.544192.

PART II

Religion contributing to violence against women and girls

2

ORIENTATION

The role of religion in contributing to violence against women and girls and its consequences

Sandra Iman Pertek and Elisabet le Roux

In Part II we examine the role of religion in shaping vulnerability to violence against women and girls (VAWG) and potentially in undermining attempts to address VAWG and its consequences. In Chapter 3, Le Roux focused on Christian communities and in Chapter 4, Pertek engaged with Muslim communities. Both chapters are based on the exploratory research work of the authors to identify ways in which religion can play to compound risks to violence and hinder recovery of survivors and victims. This section ends with a reflection chapter in which we summarise key learning points from the preceding chapters.

Conceptual framework: Religious resources in contributing to VAWG

As set out in the Introduction, this book is structured using Ter Haar's four religious resources as a framework. In this section we use the four resources to outline how religion, as a risk factor, may drive VAWG.

DOI: 10.4324/9781003169086-4

Religious ideas can undermine women's safety and be (mis) used by perpetrators and survivors/victims to legitimise abusive behaviours (Carlson, 2005), in particular by referring to patriarchal religious interpretations to justify abuse in the domestic sphere. Religious narrations have been historically interpreted in ambiguous ways favouring men and shaping power imbalances that disadvantaged women. Ghafournia (2017) in her study with Muslim survivors in Australia, however, highlights that "It was not the patriarchal precepts of religion but the patriarchal interpretation that facilitated the abuse" (p. 159). Patriarchal interpretations can lead survivors to isolation, self-blame, emotional abuse, coercion, intimidation and fear (Alkahteeb, n.d.; Safe Haven, 2014).

Religious beliefs can also restrain help-seeking of women subjected to abuse. In various religious traditions, guarding one's 'purity' before marriage or even keeping limited contact with the opposite sex is important, and for survivors who are religious, an experience of VAWG may lead to the belief that they are not abiding by these principles. In Kamau's (2016) study of rape survivors in Kenya, religious women who were sexually abused, reported feelings of guilt and fear of ridicule for being impure due to sexual relations before marriage. Survivors may believe in the sanctity of marriage, the husband's leadership role and the woman's role as an obedient wife and mother (Chavis and Hill, 2008). Also, spiritual struggles, for example, perceiving violence as God's punishment or abandonment, may exacerbate mental health conditions. Abused religious women may endure their predicament with the idea that 'this life does not matter', awaiting a better life hereafter (Hassouneh-Phillips, 2003:688; Chavis and Hill, 2008). Also, intimate-partner violence is often seen as a private problem in faith communities which may be underpinned by religious beliefs that a woman cannot refuse intimacy with her husband, rejecting the possibility of rape in marriage. The religious belief in 'marital rights' can be used to argue that marital rape does not exist within the framework of reciprocal marital responsibilities, in which a husband is permitted to demand intimate relationships with his spouse (Heise et al., 1996).

Religious practices influence survivors' meanings and experiences of VAWG. Socially constructed understandings of religious practices have often been accused of condoning VAWG. For example, FGM/C (female genital mutilation and/or cutting) occurs in religious communities of various religious affiliations which may misconstrue FGM/C as a religious practice, even though it may not be mentioned in the religious scripture. For example, the Qur'an has no reference to FGM/C, but some Muslim communities, that may erroneously connote FGM/C with religion, refer to the several contested *hadiths*, that are mostly weak or inauthentic to justify this practice. In contrast, scholars can demystify these Islamic sources to help delink FGM/C from Islam (e.g. Lethome Asmani and Abdi, 2008). Likewise, the religious convictions and norms related to minimum age of marriage may have an impact on parents' decisions and religious leaders allowing the union with a minor without capacity to consent (Pertek and Abdulaziz, 2018). Again, religious actors have a potential to counter such narratives with contextualised religious literacy.

Religious organisation and communities can also indirectly and silently collaborate in perpetrating abuse. In many faith communities VAWG and concepts linked to sexual and reproductive health and rights are particularly sensitive issues (Tomkins et al., 2015). Some victims may refrain from seeking help because of the taboo linked to discussing intimate relations. Extreme stigma around VAWG survivors in faith communities intensifies psychological trauma of victims. Survivors/victims tend to avoid discussing sensitive issues as they perceive that culture or religion disallows to tackle difficult and private issues (Kulwicki et al., 2010). For example, the study of Pavlish et al. (2010) with Somali immigrant women, identified several taboo issues, such as sex before marriage and abortion, as issues considered by them as inappropriate for discussion.

Literature well recognises faith leaders' ability to affect social acceptance and tolerance of VAWG or build resistance to it in communities. In the ecological framework of violence, religious institutions and ideologies are considered as part of structural factors that have the power to influence micro, meso and macro levels

(Heise, 1998). Although women victims tend to rely on religious leaders more often than other professionals (Singletary, 2007), religious leaders can also act as barriers to victims' safety and compound their vulnerability by advising abused women to endure violence with patience (Kulwicki et al., 2010; Le Roux et al., 2016; Ghafournia, 2017).

Religious/spiritual experience – the spiritual events, feelings and emotions – shape the context and reality in which VAWG occurs. Religious experience may distort judgement of survivors and become a source of vulnerability to further harm through interpretations of night-time dreams, feelings and realisation of their prayers. Religious experience, similarly as religious beliefs, may encourage victims to endure abuse and belittle harm as a sacrifice and promise of live hereafter (Chavis and Hill, 2008). Victims may wish to emulate the suffering of their Prophets and role models mentioned in religious scriptures, minimising their own suffering. For example, Mahoney et al. (2015) looked at women's spiritual struggles and resources which have respectively hindered leaving abusive relationships but facilitated acceptance through spiritual and religion-based reappraisal.

Overview of Part 2

In writing Le Roux's Chapter 3, "A Christian perspective: Religion contributing to VAWG and its consequences", the author engaged in an inductive analysis process with data from 14 different studies she was involved in over the past 12 years. While in the chapter reference is made to a number of these studies (and some short examples and quotes also included), Chapter 3 uses extensive examples and illustrations from only three of the studies. As these three studies are engaged with in more detail, a brief overview of the background, aim and methodology of each is offered here. The three studies were conducted with ethical clearance from Stellenbosch University's Research Ethics Committee: Humanities.

In 2010, Le Roux conducted explorative research for Tearfund UK on the role of African Christian churches in addressing sexual violence against women in conflict-affected settings (Le Roux, 2010, 2014). The study was conducted in three areas affected by armed conflict (the Democratic Republic of Congo, Rwanda and Liberia), using a qualitative, multiple-case study approach and thematic analysis. In two sites in each country (one urban and one rural), structured interview questionnaires, semi-structured interviews and nominal groups were conducted, focusing on the causes and consequences of sexual violence against women and how it is being addressed, specifically by churches. A total of 244 people took part in these sessions (68 in the DRC, 79 in Rwanda and 97 in Liberia).

A 2018 study, commissioned by Girls Not Brides, focused on the role of resistant religious leaders in efforts to end child marriage (Le Roux and Palm, 2018). The study included a literature review and 15 key informant interviews (KIIs) conducted virtually with practitioners who have experience of engaging with Christian, Muslim and/or Hindu religious leaders on child marriage. Thematic analysis was done.

In 2018–2019, Episcopal Relief and Development commissioned a study that explored how and why members of the Anglican Mothers' Union in Zambia (MUZ) contribute to and/or challenge violence against women and violence against children (Le Roux and Palm, 2018). The decision was made to focus the research within the MUZ as it has a unique and highly influential role in the Anglican Church and in the lives of women in the wider church and community. A qualitative approach was used, including an adapted form of Photovoice as the central method of data collection, and thematic analysis done of the data collected. Two hundred and thirty-eight photos and 238 voicenotes were collected by the research participants. Aside from the photos and voicenotes collected as part of the Photovoice process, 18 key informant interviews (KIIs) were conducted with key leaders within the Zambian Anglican Church and Mothers' Union as well as eight KIIs with the participants and assistants involved in the Photovoice roll-out. Nine focus group discussions were conducted by two research assistants, with members of the MUZ, future members of the MUZ, and with non-members of the MUZ.

In Pertek's Chapter 4, "A Muslim perspective: Religion as intersecting risk in VAWG", the author adopts a social constructivist and intersectional perspective in her exploratory and qualitative studies conducted as part of a PhD project in Turkey and Tunisia (2018–2021) (Pertek, 2022a; 2022b). She also draws upon her work experience, at the time as Senior Policy Advisor on Gender for Islamic Relief Worldwide (2014–2018), responsible for the development of a gender policy (IRW, 2015) and gender integration strategy in international programmes as well as her involvement in a gender study and pilot gender-based violence (GBV) project with Islamic Relief Ethiopia. In Chapter 4 itself, she predominantly uses examples and accounts from Turkey and Ethiopia.

Pertek's study in Turkey aimed to understand the religious influences on experiences of intersectional violence among forced migrant women survivors of gendered violence. The study, using an integrated intersectional and ecological analysis, explored the intersection of VAWG, religion and forced displacement to identify how religion shapes displaced survivors' vulnerability and resilience to the continuum of gendered violence. The methods involved in-depth and semi-structured interviews allowing respondents to control the pace of interviews and for unexpected but productive digression (Gubrium et al., 2012). Local and skilled interpreters supported the interviews in Arabic. The sample included Muslim women residing in Turkey, Ankara: 21 from Syria and 2 from Iraq (collectively called in the Chapter 'Levantine women'). All respondents were survivors of multiple forms of violence and discrimination, including domestic and extended family violence, sexual harassment and racism experienced across the continuum of forced migration, from pre-displacement, conflict, flight and into refuge. Respondents spoke about religion in response to questions concerning their experiences of abuse and the role of religion in their vulnerability and discrimination.

Also, key informant interviews (KIIs) were conducted online and in person with 16 practitioners who worked on VAWG/GBV in local and international organisations across different regions. Throughout the research, great attention was paid to ethical considerations with regard to working with relatively vulnerable social groups (forced migrant populations and survivors of violence) on sensitive topics to ensure no harm was caused and emotional risks were minimised by a survivor-centred research procedure. Also, the safety of the researcher and interpreters was prioritised by limiting the number of interviews conducted each day and by following a security protocol. Ethical approval was acquired from the University of Birmingham Humanities and Social Sciences Ethical Review Committee. All data was anonymised and pseudonyms were used throughout the chapter.

With the gender study conducted in 2015 in Ethiopia, Pertek did a case study in the remote, nomadic and rural areas of the Somali Regional State in Ethiopia, Dekasuftu Woreda. The study was part of efforts to develop gender policy and VAWG programming on behalf of a faith-inspired humanitarian agency. The study aimed to understand gender dynamics, gender roles, access to and control over resources, gender needs and protection concerns in selected localities receiving humanitarian aid. Methods involved five sex segregated and one mixed focus group discussions (FGDs) with community members, two workshops with staff, as well as ten key informant interviews with community leaders and service providers, such as local authorities, NGO staff, local imam, teacher and health workers. Pertek's empirical chapter draws upon the FGDs, KIIs, research field notes, observations and workshop outcomes with staff and project reports of Islamic Relief Ethiopia's (IRE) integrated VAWG intervention implemented in 2016–2017 (IRE cited in Pertek, 2020).

Both Pertek's PhD study and gender assessment used an inductive approach and thematic analysis to derive key themes discussed herein. Systematic thematic analysis was used because it is a flexible method of qualitative analysis which fits well within a social constructivist paradigm which can "*provide a rich and detailed, yet complex account of data*" (Braun and Clarke, 2006:78).

Part II concludes with Chapter 5 ("Joint reflections on religion countering VAWG"), which uses the two preceding chapters as a starting point for a general reflection on the negative aspects of the intersections between religion and VAWG.

References

Alkahteeb, S. (n.d.). *Muslim wheel of domestic violence.* Viewed from http://www.stopfamilyviolencenow.org/Portals/0/tools/Wheel-Domestic_Violence.pdf [Date accessed: August 10, 2018].

Braun, V. and Clarke, V. (2006). Using thematic analysis in psychology. *Qualitative Research in Psychology*, 3 (2): 77–101. doi:10.1191/14780 88706qp063oa.

Carlson, S. (2005). "Contesting and reinforcing patriarchy: An analysis of domestic violence in the Dzaleka refugee camp", RSC Working Paper No. 23. University of Oxford. Viewed from https://www.rsc.ox.ac.uk/files/files-1/wp23-contesting-reinforcing-patriarchy-2005.pdf [Date accessed: May 10, 2018].

Chavis, A.Z. and Hill, M.S. (2008). "Integrating multiple intersecting identities: A multicultural conceptualization of the power and control wheel", *Women & Therapy*, 32(1): 121–149. doi:10.1080/0270 3140802384552.

Ghafournia, N. (2017). "Muslim women and domestic violence: Developing a framework for social work practice", *Journal of Religion & Spirituality in Social Work: Social Thought*, 36(1–2): 146–163. doi:10.1080/15426432.2017.1313150.

Gubrium, J., Holstein, J., Marvasti, A. and McKinney, K. (2012). *The SAGE handbook of interview research: The complexity of the craft*. Newbury Park, CA: SAGE Publications, Inc.

Hassouneh-Phillips, D. (2003). "Strength and vulnerability: Spirituality in abused American Muslim women's lives", *Issues in Mental Health Nursing*, 24(6–7): 681–694. doi:10.1080/01612840305324.

Heise, L. (1998). "Violence against women: An integrated, ecological framework", *Violence against Women*, 4(3): 262–290. doi:10.1177/1077 801298004003002.

Heise, L., Moore, K. and Toubia, N. (1996). "Defining 'coercion' and 'consent' cross-culturally", *SIECUS Report*, 24(2): 12–14.

IRW. (2015). *Gender justice policy*. Birmingham: Islamic Relief Worldwide.

Kamau, J.W. (2016). "Female survivors of sexual violence: Cultural and socio-economic factors that influence first visits to the SGBV clinics at Kenyatta national hospital", MSc Thesis, University of Nairobi. Viewed from http://erepository.uonbi.ac.ke/handle/11295/98486 [Date accessed: May 10, 2021].

Kulwicki, A., Aswad, B., Carmona, T. and Ballout, S. (2010). "Barriers in the utilization of domestic violence services among Arab immigrant women: Perceptions of professionals, service providers & community leaders", *Journal of Family Violence*, 25, 727–735. doi:10.1007/s10896-010-9330–8.

Le Roux, E. (2010). *An explorative baseline: The role of the church in sexual violence in countries that are/were in armed conflict, in a preventative sense and as a caring institution*. London: Tearfund.

Le Roux, E. (2014). "The role of African Christian Churches in dealing with sexual violence against women: The case of the democratic Republic of Congo, Rwanda and Liberia", PhD Dissertation, Stellenbosch University.

Le Roux, E., Kramm, N., Scott, N., Sandilands, M., Loots, L., Olivier, J., Arango, D. and O'Sullivan, V. (2016). "Getting dirty: Working with faith leaders to prevent and respond to gender-based violence", *The Review of Faith & International Affairs*, 14(3): 22–35. doi:10.1080/15570 274.2016.1215837.

Le Roux, E. and Palm, S. (2018). *What lies beneath? Tackling the roots of religious resistance to ending child marriage.* Girls not Brides. Viewed from https://www.girlsnotbrides.org/learning-resources/resource-centre/ what-lies-beneath-tackling-the-roots-of-religious-resistance-to-ending-child-marriage-2/ [Date accessed: April 6, 2022].

Lethome Asmani, I. and Abdi, M. (2008). *Delinking female genital mutilation/cutting from Islam.* Population Council. doi:10.31899/rh14.1025.

Mahoney, A., Abadi, L. and Pargament, K.I. (2015). "Exploring women's spiritual struggles and resources to cope with intimate partner aggression", in A.J. Johnson (ed.), *Religion and men's violence against women.* New York, NY: Springer, 45–59. doi:10.1007/978-1-4939-2266-6_4.

Pavlish, C.L., Noor, S. and Brandt, J. (2010). "Somali immigrant women and the American health care system: Discordant beliefs, divergent expectations, and silent worries", *Social Science & Medicine*, 71(2): 353–361. doi:10.1016/j.socscimed.2010.04.010.

Pertek, S.I. (2020). "Deconstructing Islamic perspectives on sexual and gender-based violence (GBV), toward a faith inclusive approach", in A.A. Khan and A. Cheema (eds.), *Islam and International Development: Insights for working with Muslim communitie*s. Rugby, UK: Practical Action Publishing, 131–152.

Pertek, S.I. (2022a). "Religion, forced migration and the continuum of violence: An intersectional and ecological analysis". PhD Dissertation, University of Birmingham.

Pertek, S.I. (2022b). "'God helped us': Resilience, religion and experiences of gender-based violence and trafficking among African forced migrant women", *Social Sciences*, 11(5): 201. doi:10.3390/socsci11050201.

Pertek, S.I. and Abdulaziz, S. (2018). *Don't force me: A policy brief on early and forced marriage.* Birmingham, UK: Islamic Relief Worldwide. Viewed from http://www.islamic-relief.org/wp-content/uploads/2018/03/ FORCED-MARRIAGE-CSW62.pdf [Date accessed: April 16, 2018].

Safe Havens. (2014). *Spiritual abuse wheel.* Safe Havens Interfaith Partnership Against Domestic Violence. Viewed from https://www.

livingwatersofhope.org/spiritual-abuse-wheel/ [Date accessed: May 20, 2020].

Singletary, J. (2007). "Family violence in congregations: An exploratory study of Clergy's needs", *Social Work and Christianity*, 34: 18–46.

Tomkins, A., Duff, J., Fitzgibbon, A., Karam, A., Mills, E.J., Munnings, K., Smith, S., Seshadri, S.R., Steinberg, A., Vitillo, R. and Yugi, P. (2015). "Controversies in faith and health care", *The Lancet*, 386(10005): 1776–1785. doi: 10.1016/S0140–6736(15)60252-5.

3

A CHRISTIAN PERSPECTIVE

Religion contributing to violence against women and girls and its consequences

Elisabet le Roux

Introduction

> At the baptismal class at my church, they asked me if I have a
> husband. I said no. I did not say anything else. I did not want to
> explain it to them (why I had a child and no husband)… I did not
> want to tell them what happened to me, because they do not do
> anything for survivors.
>
> (Survivor, Liberia, interview in 2010)

This chapter explores how Christian religious actors challenge
violence against women and girls (VAWG) prevention and response.
While this chapter was written after engaging in an inductive
analysis process with data from 14 different studies, I use extensive examples and illustrations from only three of these studies in
this chapter (for more information and methodological detail on
these three studies, please see Chapter 2). Relying on Ter Haar's
four categories of religious resources as a conceptual framework for
this exploration, I first engage with the complex entanglement of
religion and culture, and how this drives VAWG. Second, I look at
how the avoidance and vilification of sex and sexuality is in itself

DOI: 10.4324/9781003169086-5

a religious practice that is harmful but also drives other practices harmful to women and girls. Third, I explore the patriarchal nature of church organisations and how this drives VAWG and the inability to adequately address it. Finally, I explore how certain religious experiences fundamentally challenge VAWG prevention and response.

Religious ideas: The entanglement of religion and culture

Whereas many Christians claim that their religious ideas, or the content of their belief, is divinely inspired and required, the reality is that religion and culture are entangled in complex ways. Religious ideas are often heavily influenced by culture and in turn influence culture. Various studies I have been involved in have highlighted how emmeshed religion and culture are, and how these complex connections contribute to the continued perpetration of VAWG.

In research conducted in 2018–2019 within the Anglican Mothers' Union in Zambia (MUZ), we looked at how and why members of the MUZ contribute to and/or challenge violence against women and violence against children. A recurring theme in the data was the complex entanglement of religion and culture. Various harmful beliefs and practices were identified and explained as caused and/or justified by both religion and culture. What was interesting, however, is that the different research assistants, interviewees and focus group participants differed on the primary agent – religion or culture. For example, everyone agreed that there is a strong belief that women should keep the secrets of their households, including when they are being abused by their husbands. But some informants ascribed this belief to culture: "It's a cultural thing… It's like (what happens in a) marriage should be a secret. The relationship should be a secret" (Female religious leader, Zambia, interview in 2018). Other informants explained that it is Christianity that demands this silence and secrecy: "… the religious belief that you cannot talk about this because (you) are Christians, you're going to embarrass your husband…" (Male religious leader,

Zambia, interview in 2019). Then there were informants that explained that both religion and culture drive and justify the same harmful belief. For example, a cultural belief – captured in the idiom 'the man cannot break the home' – dictates that a husband's infidelities cannot lead to divorce, whereas a woman's infidelities automatically end the marriage. Many informants explained that their religion teaches the same principle, emphasising the importance of female fidelity and the right that husbands have to extramarital affairs. Therefore, while informants easily identified and discussed how religion and culture drive certain beliefs that may harm women and girls, there were conflicting views on the 'original' source of the belief.

The reading and interpretation of the Bible is another illustration of how interdependent culture and religion are. Depending on the setting, the Bible can be quoted and interpreted to support various forms of VAWG, such as wife beating, marital rape, and widow inheritance, but also beliefs that limit women and girls' equality and independent decision-making, such as on the use of contraception and decisions on family size. For example, Ephesians 5:22–24 is often quoted in support of women's submissiveness to men's headship and decision-making power ("Wives, submit to your own husbands, as to the Lord... (N)ow as the church submits to Christ, so also wives should submit in everything to their husbands"); a wife's inability to refuse sex is justified through 1 Corinthians 11:3 ("...for the wife does not have authority over her own body, but the husband does"), while the sinfulness of divorce is supported by Matthew 19:3–9 ("What therefore God has joined together, let no man separate"). Of course, alternative interpretations of these scriptures, which do not marginalise and discriminate against women, are also available. For example, Ephesians 5:22–24, when read in relation to the entire Chapter 5, is interpreted as calling for the mutual, loving submission of both husband and wife to each other (Lovše, 2009). Furthermore, other scriptures can be used to argue for women's equality and right to refuse sex and leave a marriage. For example, Galatians 3:28 is quoted to support gender equality: "There is neither Jew nor Gentile, neither slave nor free, nor is there male and female, for you are all one in Christ Jesus". So why are certain scriptures and interpretations selected in some churches and not in others? Musimbi Kanyoro, amongst others, argues that the choice of scripture and the type of interpretation is heavily influenced by culture:

> It was through reading the Bible with women in my village for a very long time that I came to the realization of the importance of culture in people's live and the consequent influence of that culture on the interpretation of the Bible.
>
> *(Kanyoro, 2001:42)*

The entanglement of religion and culture has emerged in a number of studies looking at religion and/or VAWG (e.g. Kanyoro, 2001; Bradley, 2010; Greiff, 2010; Myambo, 2018). In my own research, this entanglement is especially obvious where religious ideas are used to justify harmful practices that many understand as cultural practices. For example, Biblical evidence that Mary, the mother of Jesus, was married as a child is used as a religious justification for child marriage (Le Roux and Palm, 2018); the Biblical emphasis on purity and chastity until marriage is used to justify female genital mutilation and cutting (FGM/C) (Le Roux and Bartelink, 2017); and Biblical calls to be a 'good wife' is used to justify husbands' complaints to their pastors if a wife does not submit to labia elongation (Palm et al., 2017). Some religious actors may argue that religion does not require such harmful practices and that such religious justifications were only added to cultural practices 'after the fact'. Nevertheless, the reality is that religion and religious ideas are playing a role in the continued perpetration of many harmful practices. For example, as an interviewee explained from her work on child marriage in Brazil:

> Some families told us that 'actually, I didn't want to marry my girl [sic] but I felt fear about my religious leader's reaction and my community's religious reaction. And then I understand it (as) better for my girl to take this marriage [sic]'...
>
> *(Female researcher, quoted in Le Roux and Palm, 2018:8)*

Religious actors at times refute such examples by explaining that this is not 'true' religion. For example, in Zambia, a number of research assistants argued that it was cultural teachings that were bringing gender inequality and VAWG into Christian couples' relationships: "...this teaching of tradition and then they're mixing (it) with Christianity, which is not good. So these teachings are bringing problems into our lives" (Female research assistant, Zambia, interview in 2019). The view is that, if religion could be purified and stripped of its cultural taint, then such harmful beliefs and practices will no longer be promoted or condoned within religious spaces. However, is this a valid argument? For there are also many examples of religion negatively impacting culture, influencing it in such a way that it becomes more harmful to women and girls. For example, ancient Judaic practices as recorded in the Bible has influenced cultures in southern Nigeria (and other non-Muslim parts of the country) to the extent that women are now required to marry within their faither's clan, and gender-differentiated access to land and property has become the norm (Para-Mallam, 2006). Christian missionaries in Africa were complicit in changing the pre-colonial gender relations, using Biblical scriptures to promote women's cultural insubordination (Van Klinken, 2013). For example, a literal interpretation of the story of Adam and Eve was used to cement the belief in women's inferiority in relation to men and women's acceptance of this oppression (Njoh and Akiwumi, 2012), and Uchem (2003) notes how the colonial Christian educational system in Nigeria served to limit women to domestic roles in marriage, which was a foreign concept in Igboland where women originally functioned on an equal status with men in the public and private sphere.

Therefore, I argue that attempts to identify the 'real' culprit in VAWG – religion or culture – ignore the reality that religion and culture are inherently entangled and mutually influence each other. Maluleke and Nadar (2002) have drawn attention to how this entanglement drives VAWG, identifying religion, culture and gender socialisation as a "unholy trinity" (Maluleke and Nadar, 2002:14). To try to argue which one was first responsible for ideas harmful to women and girls is the same as arguing about whether the chicken or the egg came first! Some authors conceptualise this entanglement by viewing religion as a cultural expression; others explain that belonging to a particular religion inherently means belonging to a particular culture (Beyers, 2017). Speaking specifically of African Christians, Kanyoro (2001) argues that

> the notion that it is possible and desirable to live by the gospel without culture is a belief held with much wishful thinking.... In the African indigenous thought system, culture and religion are not distinct from each other. Therefore, culture and religion in Africa embrace all areas of one's total life. There is no sphere of existence that is excluded from the double grip of culture and religion.
>
> *(Kanyoro, 2001:36)*

In reflecting on the content of religious belief and how it links to VAWG, this discussion serves to highlight that religious ideas are not independent, stand-alone, divinely inspired notions. Religion and culture are each in itself influenced and formed by the other. In terms of VAWG prevention and response, the relationship between religion and culture, and how it links to VAWG, becomes more than a theoretical argument. A binary approach hampers VAWG prevention and response efforts as it allows for blame-shifting, where religious actors can deny the role of religion in VAWG by placing all the blame on culture. Furthermore, a binary understanding of religion and culture means that prevention and response efforts are not holistic. By focusing only on religion, there is only engagement with one component of what is driving harmful beliefs within a community. Where religion and culture are emmeshed, VAWG prevention and response measures should be able to respond to this entangled complexity.

Religious practice: Avoiding and vilifying sex and sexuality

In 2010 I conducted research in three countries (the Democratic Republic of Congo [DRC], Rwanda and Liberia) affected by armed conflict, on the role of African Christian churches in addressing and responding to sexual violence against women. In the course of the fieldwork, a picture emerged of churches (of different denominations) that not only avoid addressing and responding to sexual violence but also generally avoid all sex-related matters. This was often explained as part of a broader cultural taboo around talking about sex, as was explained by a (male) leader from the DRC: "In Africa talking about sex is a taboo, it is very difficult. Even in households and churches, to talk about sex and sexual intercourse is still a taboo" (quoted in Le Roux, 2014:118). Since then, I have found this same resistance to talking about sex or sex-related matters within Christian churches belonging to different denominations (including catholic, protestant, evangelical, pentecostal and orthodox) and amongst different Christian religious leaders in many different countries. This avoidance facilitates various harmful practices and, I argue, is actually in itself a type of (harmful) religious practice. Below I discuss how the religious practice of avoiding sex and sex-related matters, and even vilifying it, in different ways drive VAWG and challenges VAWG prevention and response.

What many churches teach about sex and relationships can lead to VAWG. First, teachings (e.g. in sermons) tend to instate a strong gender hierarchy, firmly placing men in control of women, the relationship and sex. Drawing on Biblical scriptures (e.g. Ephesians 5, 1 Corinthians 11 and Colossians 3) the headship of the husband and the submissiveness of the wife are emphasised. At times there is recognition that the power imbalance may put women at risk of violence. Yet often, rather than address and transform the risky relationship dynamic, women are taught how to navigate these risks and dangers. For example, in Rwanda, a female leader of a prominent women's organisation within a church explained that they teach women to be humble before their husbands, how to avoid being forced if they do not want to have sex, but to also work hard to become financially self-sufficient. In other words, the power imbalances are not challenged, but women are rather taught how to make themselves less vulnerable to it:

> What we teach, there are some men who want to do sexual relations by force. Even though they are married, but they do

it by force. We teach the women, how to care and to handle those men… (We teach women in church) to be humble before (their husbands), to obey them, to work hard in order to get your own means, so that you need not ask him 'give me, give me, give me'… (And) the way (we) teach women, it is a process (to refuse sex). The way you treat him when he comes home, the way you share a meal, until you go to sleep. So that, when you reach that point (that you refuse sex) it will be okay (and he will not force you to have sex).

(Female church leader, Rwanda, 2010, quoted in Le Roux,
2014:153)

However, it is not only unequal power dynamics that are being promoted in many churches. Often churches require that survivors stay silent about the violence they experience. This may be described as a way of 'saving the soul' of the abusive partner and/or portraying the violence being experienced as a religious martyrdom. Disclosing the violence would then be selfish and upset God's plans. Often, Biblical scriptures are used to convince the abused to stay within the abusive relationship. The normalisation of these kinds of narratives was particularly clear in the research conducted with the Anglican MUZ. A strong narrative existed that MUZ members must keep the secrets of their household no matter what the circumstances. Any form of abuse (including abuse of children) must therefore not be disclosed to anyone:

Because in the Mothers' Union it is believed that you have to keep secrets. Whatever is happening to you in your home, you don't have to disclose to anyone. It is just between you and your husband. And also when my husband hits me, then it is a sign of love.

(Female research assistant, Zambia, 2019, quoted in Le Roux &
Palm, 2019:50)

Furthermore, the MUZ is also strongly opposed to divorce. As disclosure of VAWG may lead to divorce, it should therefore not be done. As explained by a MUZ member in 2018:

So these policies are laid out. We follow them. Even when you are beaten, (or) he comes in the early hours (after being with another woman) – you just open the door. That is the counsel we were given (by the Mothers' Union).

(quoted in Le Roux & Palm, 2019:51)

In the DRC, the same narrative was present, as a male leader of a non-governmental organisation (NGO) explained in 2010: "(I)f someone is victim of domestic violence and she wants a pastor to help, the pastor would say 'no, you don't talk about your domestic violence.' Because it is a household secret" (quoted in Le Roux, 2014:117). In the DRC, Rwanda and Liberia, various informants experienced their churches as seeing sex, and anything related to it, as not being religious matters and therefore not appropriate for discussion within religious spaces or with religious leaders. At best, a religious leader may counsel or pray for a survivor, but there is no concerted effort to address VAWG and assist survivors:

Survivors do not get any material support from any church. Churches are maybe saying sexual violence is wrong. But churches are not doing any marches, or taking any stand against it. There is nothing big, no great effort, no seriousness.

(Male church leader, Liberia, 2010, quoted in Le Roux, 2014:184)

This practice of refusing to talk about sex, sexual violence and VAWG generally, or to do so in a limited manner, has wider implications. A space that does not talk about VAWG often becomes a stigmatising and discriminatory space for those who have experienced VAWG. When women and girls disclose the violence they experience, they are not enduring in silence as is expected. In the DRC, Rwanda and Liberia many of the survivors I interviewed had not disclosed to anyone in their churches, for they did not see any benefit to doing so. On the contrary, they fear stigma and discrimination from people in their congregation and the wider community. This is a legitimate fear, for a number of the survivors that have disclosed to people in their churches are now being stigmatised. One survivor from Rwanda (interviewed in 2010) explained her experience as follows: "Instead of encouraging me, providing moral support, church members from (my) church they talk, they (gossip), they want to spend a long time talking about what happened to me. They are not supportive. They do nothing". Some churches even force survivors to reconcile with their perpetrators. In Rwanda, this appeared to be more common with survivors that experienced sexual violence during the genocide. Again, the call for forgiveness is packaged as ensuring the salvation of the perpetrator:

> There are some churches who don't accept that (survivors testify against their perpetrators). They force them to forgive those who raped them, which is not good. That forgiveness should come from the heart, not by force… (They tell them that) if they keep quiet, those (perpetrators) will be saved.
> *(Female NGO leader, Rwanda, 2010, quoted in Le Roux, 2014:154)*

Some churches and church leaders (including clergy at various levels) are also promoting certain practices that are harmful to women and girls. Religious support for these practices is often due to religious ideals around virginity, sexual purity, chastity and fidelity. For example, Leviticus 21:13–14 emphasises the importance of men marrying virgin women, while Ephesians 5:3 and 1 Thessalonians 4:3–4 denounce sexual immorality. In the light of such religious ideals, harmful practices such as child marriage and FGM/C are fairly consistently explained as a way to ensure the sexual purity of girls and to prevent them from having extramarital pregnancies (El-Damanhoury, 2013; Le Roux and Palm, 2018). Even if these practices may have some harmful consequences, these consequences are seen as less harmful than what is perceived as the greatest sin, namely being sexually impure. In such settings, sex becomes sinful and virginity, chastity and fidelity become key religious virtues to be defended at all costs. Practices that ensure these virtues are then justifiable. For example, child marriage is a practice supported by many Christian communities as a way of avoiding extramarital sexual relations. As a development practitioner shared during a study on religious leaders and harmful practices, many Christians in Mali (as one example) see child marriage as a fully justifiable practice, called for by their religion's prioritisation of purity and virginity:

> (The Christian community complains that) everyone's talking about how wrong (child marriage) is, but why are we not talking about how wrong early pregnancy (is, or) early sexual activity. So that's what they were saying, so kind of saying "we'll marry our girls because, you know, we want them to be protected from all of these, you know, premature sexual acts."
>
> *(Development practitioner, quoted in Le Roux and Bartelink, 2017:6)*

There appears to be a fundamental discomfort within many Christian religious spaces with sex and sexuality. This often means that sex and sexuality are avoided, feared and even vilified and can lead to the religious promotion of practices that can 'control' sex and sexuality. At the very least, Christian religious spaces may demand that sex and sexuality only be practised within religiously ordained spaces: a marriage relationship, for the enjoyment of the man. It may also mean that anything related to sex and sexuality – including speaking about VAWG – is avoided and deemed 'unreligious'. Such religious spaces and leaders that avoid talking about sex and vilify sex and sexuality challenges VAWG prevention and response efforts. It challenges not only prevention (as you cannot talk about sex and sexuality) but also response (for you cannot actually name and discuss many of the consequences of VAWG). Furthermore, if virginity and chastity are prioritised to the detriment of other considerations, religious spaces become unsafe spaces for survivors of sexual violence.

Religious organisation: The entanglement of religion and patriarchy

Within VAWG as a field of research and theorising, 'patriarchy' has long been a prominent concept, useful in highlighting the distinct arrangements between genders (Kandiyoti, 1988). Patriarchy can be defined as "social arrangements that privilege males, where men as a group dominate women as a group, both structurally and ideologically—hierarchical arrangements that manifest in varieties across history and social space" (Hunnicutt, 2009:557). As such it is both a result and a driver of gender inequality and takes on different forms in different societies and at different times (Hunnicutt, 2009). Especially radical feminism has been heavily critical of patriarchy, calling for fundamental change in those structures of society that are embedded in patriarchy and hegemonic masculinity.

While linking violence and patriarchy has faced criticism, it remains relevant as it allows explanations of VAWG to focus on gendered social arrangements and power (Hunnicutt, 2009; Barker, 2016). Looking through the lens of patriarchy reveals how violence is based on complex power relations (Barker, 2016). Some authors have even called for the need to refer to 'patriarchal violence' (rather than 'male violence') in order to provide an analytical and political framework that can adequately account for the power differential present in violence. Furthermore, such framing can help to highlight that violence by men is not a natural or normal part of manhood, nor only a function of gender, but also a result of power (Barker, 2016).

The research conducted in 2010 in the DRC, Rwanda and Liberia revealed how local Christian churches (including catholic, protestant, evangelical and pentecostal denominations) promote and support patriarchal beliefs and practices. As such, they not only struggle to address VAWG but also are fundamental to the patriarchal project that helps drive VAWG. This finding has since been confirmed in many of the studies I was part of in other countries and contexts. Churches, as religious organisations, in terms of how they are constructed and empowered are inherently prone to directly and indirectly promoting VAWG. A good illustration of this is the 2010 research in the DRC, Rwanda and Liberia.

I asked 15 people (all older than 18 years) in each community I did research with the same question during key informant interviews: Are men and women equal in your community, and why do you say so? Across all communities and countries the answer was quite consistent: no, they are not. Men are more important and powerful than women: "They are unequal. In meetings, men are recognised, but women do not have a voice" (Woman, Liberia, interview in 2010); "It is culturally ordained, for it is a husband that takes you from your home to his home. So, the woman becomes dependent on him and that is why he is superior" (Woman, DRC, interview in 2010); "Normally men and women are not equal in this community. The reason why they are not equal is because some are powerful. Men have power, women are not powerful as men are" (Man, Rwanda, interview in 2010). While female informants did not necessarily always agree with the status quo, often pointing out that they do most of the work and should therefore be more important than men, they nevertheless reported that their communities see and treat men as superior to women. While some informants referred to 'new' ideas (usually from NGOs) about gender equality or how the Bible states that all are created in God's image, the dominant narrative was still of the man as head of the household, making decisions and dictating to the household. Where there have been efforts to promote gender equality, there may even be push-back from men who are eager to ensure their continued control, as explained by a woman from Rwanda:

> Nowadays there is a specific reason which push[es] men to abuse their wives, because they say 'ah, there is a gender sensitive issue in this country and ... you say that we are all equal, I want to show you how we are not equal...' It is done by the men to show, 'even though you are attending the training session, I want to show you that we are not equal.'
> *(Woman, Rwanda, 2010, quoted in Le Roux, 2014:146)*

Male and female community leaders (almost all of them also church members) condemned what they saw as churches' non-involvement in addressing VAWG and especially sexual violence. They argued that church leaders do not see it as 'their' problem because of the power dynamic between men and women. Addressing VAWG would require investigation and transformation of patriarchal gender relations and power dynamics. Furthermore, many religious men do not actually believe that women are their equals. They therefore not only struggle with power sharing but also hold on to a deep-seated belief in the inferiority of women. As one male NGO leader in the DRC explained: "(T)he church is one of the main organisations that (is) suppressing women" (quoted in Le Roux, 2014:117). The issue of having churches join VAWG prevention and response efforts is therefore not simple at all, as it actually requires a profound transformation:

> This is a big issue, how to balance the power. We succeed when those who are church leaders accept power sharing... It is like an inheritance culture of dominant masculinity, where both Christians and those who don't believe (hold on to it)... It is inheritance and a lack of knowledge... Those who are ruling some churches or those who are local authorities are not informed correctly about the human rights, especially the rights of women and men, and they are themselves in the frontline to oppress women.
> *(Male NGO leader, DRC, 2010, quoted in Le Roux, 2014:117)*

As church leaders are usually men, they have a vested interest in not upsetting the status quo, as it empowers them. Addressing VAWG thus becomes a threat to their own power. That is why some male religious leaders (at various levels of the church hierarchy) may even actively try to undermine efforts to empower women, while others promote gender inequality and forms of VAWG. For example, stigmatising survivors can help to enforce churches' beliefs and values on the importance of virginity, purity and monogamy, and by stigmatising survivors, churches reinforce their power as ingroup and create social cohesion amongst church members (Link and Phelan, 2001; Yang et al., 2007; Link and Phelan, 2014; Le Roux, 2021). Stigmatising survivors thus becomes a way that patriarchal constructions of women, men and sex are promoted within churches, ensuring the continuation of the status quo and men's dominance.

In various countries, Christian churches have quite a good track record of addressing human rights violations, corrupt regimes, election corruption, armed conflict and of democracy building and peacebuilding (Sabar-Friedman, 1997; Péclard, 1998; Pfeiffer,

2004; Ross, 2004; Taylor, 2005; Akoko and Oben, 2006; Gifford, 2008). Therefore, there is ample evidence of their ability to challenge injustice. However, what the research in the DRC, Rwanda and Liberia showed was that this is often not the case with VAWG. Why not? I would argue that most churches fail to engage with VAWG because most churches, as organisations, are patriarchal institutions. They are not merely engaging in a few patriarchal practices borrowed from a patriarchal society, but are a key structure supporting and perpetuating patriarchy. Comprehensively addressing VAWG would mean that the patriarchal structure of churches as organisations will have to be dismantled, and this would mean a loss of power for men. With most church leaders being men and the current system benefiting men in general, there is an avoidance of the issue.

Yet, it is also important to realise that it is not only religious men that ensure the patriarchal order within churches as religious organisations. 'Formenism' is a term coined to explain the phenomenon whereby women support and perpetuate patriarchy: "For*men*ism, like masculinism, subscribes to a belief in the inherent superiority of men over women…but unlike masculinism, it is not an ideology developed and sustained by men, but constructed, endorsed, and sustained by women" (Nadar and Potgieter, 2010:143; emphasis in original). Within Christian communities this phenomenon takes the form of Christian women calling for and supporting Christian men to be the leaders within the church and household, with women as their willing subjects. Religious women's compliance and complicity in the patriarchy have been explained in different ways: (a) while they may be restricted by religion, religion also shields and protects them from broader structural forces and limitations; (b) they choose to do so, so as to strategically circumvent the other life challenges they face or (c) they actually adapt, subvert or resist official religious dogma (Avishai, 2008). While it is beyond the scope of this chapter to go into women's compliance in detail (for more on this, see Le Roux, 2019), the reality is that women in Christian communities often support the patriarchal system and resist efforts to transform it.

This was amply illustrated in research conducted within the Anglican Mother's Union in Zambia. The research revealed that the

MUZ as organisation is propagating a certain model for woman-hood, namely that a woman's true purpose and fulfilment is through marriage and motherhood, thus promoting very set gender roles and norms. Submission, humility and modest dress are important, and members are taught that the state of her household – and the members of her household – is a reflection on her as an individual. Her husband should be the head of the household and she must ensure at all times that they have a 'good' marriage. To ensure a good marriage, the MUZ teaches its members how to conduct themselves. As explained by a participant during a focus group with MUZ members:

> We discuss that the man is the head of the home. We as women should submit and listen to what our husbands have to say to us. We also counsel our wives-to-be that a woman in the home should tell the truth. (Be) (h)umble. (Have a) (l)ow voice when talking.
>
> *(MUZ member, Zambia, 2018, quoted in Le Roux & Palm, 2019:54)*

Understanding and addressing the patriarchal nature of many churches may therefore require moving beyond a simplistic approach of only working with men.

The entanglement of religion and patriarchy highlights that many churches, as organisations, are invested in the patriarchal system. Directly or indirectly these organisations are propagating beliefs, norms and practices that may directly or indirectly drive VAWG. Engaging religious organisations for VAWG prevention and response is therefore arguably not as simple as choosing to motivate them to become an 'ally'. Rather, it highlights that religious organisations can be key institutions upholding the patriarchy, and that comprehensive VAWG prevention and response will *have* to engage with this dimension of society.

Religious experience: Tensions

In 2018 I was part of a research project looking at religious leader resistance to ending child marriage, where we engaged with different organisations working in different parts of the world to end child marriage (Le Roux and Palm, 2018). One organisation we spoke with was the Apostolic Women Empowerment Trust (AWET) in Zimbabwe, an inter-apostolic faith-based organisation that aims to advance the rights of adolescents and women and mainstream gender in the Apostolic Church's activities. Our informant explained that AWET has to use different approaches, depending on the specific Apostolic Church they are working with. While some Apostolic churches see the Bible as an authoritative text, and AWET's intervention efforts can therefore use certain sacred scriptures to argue against child marriage, other Apostolic communities do not see the Bible as the ultimate authority. Rather, they rely fully on the Holy Spirit. They await His communication (which may come in different forms) and when it arrives it cannot be questioned. Sometimes, specific people are chosen as regular vessels or recipients of the Holy Spirit's communications, and these people as a result have much power and influence in the religious community. Often called a Prophet, this person plays a key, authoritative role in the Apostolic community. For AWET in their child marriage intervention work, such prophets can be challenging figures to engage with, for their opinions and pronouncements cannot be questioned in any way:

> (F)or the Apostolic person, the first port of call is the Prophet. So, if the Prophet tells you something, that is what you do. So the Prophet, the Holy Spirit speaks through the Prophet, so we do not directly go and challenge what the Prophet is saying to the people through the Holy Spirit.
>
> *(AWET staff member, Zimbabwe, interviewed in 2018)*

Religious experiences – divine revelation, dreams, visions, miracles – can be a dimension of religion that the international development sphere finds difficult to engage with. While many are happy to utilise the social capital of religion (e.g. using a church as a distribution depot for food aid) there is less comfort with the unique aspects and contributions of religion and religious actors, such as religious experiences (Baker, 2012). However, these religious experiences cannot simply be dismissed, for they are real and authoritative to the members of these Christian communities. But what if a prophet states that all 12-year-old girls must be married? What if a religious leader has a dream in which God tells him that he must take all the girl children in the village as his wives? For those wishing to work with Christian communities to end VAWG, the unpredictable, unchallengeable and 'esoteric' nature of religious experience can therefore be very challenging to navigate and engage.

The reality is that religious experience can sit uncomfortably with what is seen as good practice within VAWG prevention and response. Another example is the Christian principle and experience of 'redemption'. Redemption is seen as an act of God's grace, embodied by Jesus's death on the cross, whereby He saves a person from sin and evil by suffering in the place of those who deserve to be punished (Miller, 2009:528). While there are alternative theological interpretations of the cross (e.g. where it is seen as a redemptive act for the violated and not the violator), many Christians continue to see "the Crucified only as a surrogate for the sinner who deserved punishment" (Miller, 2009:529). Such an understanding of the concept and experience of redemption may mean that Christian religious leaders face a conundrum when a member of their congregation perpetrates VAWG. Especially when the perpetrator regrets his actions, Christian leaders may be conflicted about how to respond. This tension emerged clearly in a research project that I was part of, conducted in six communities of internally displaced people in Colombia. As part of the project, church leaders from each community were asked questions on sexual violence and church responses to it. As one female pastor explained, the reality of the experience of redemptive change challenges her in her response to sexual violence:

> Because this is an important issue: Which is truly our realm as ministers? Right? Do we up and send everyone off to prison? Or do we carry out restoration processes where God can truly change people's heart? ... If we sent them all to prison we'd have I don't know how many men locked up because at one time in their life they did something. Or maybe some

women. But is that what's really going to change them? It's complicated. I mean, in these cases I really don't know what to do.

(Female faith leader, quoted in Le Roux and Cadavid Valencia,
2020:243)

The nature of religious experiences therefore challenges VAWG prevention and response in two ways. First, it is a religious resource that a non-believer may find difficult to understand or engage with. It is also deeply personal: how can you question another's dreams and visions, or his subjective experiences of transformation? Second, religious experiences may run counter to accepted VAWG prevention and response practices. For example, a religious leader may believe that a perpetrator can fundamentally change – be it through prayer or exorcism or redemption – and that this trans-formation is more important than justice measures on behalf of the victim.

Conclusion

This chapter used Ter Haar's four religious resources to guide an exploration of key ways in which Christian religious actors can, directly or indirectly, drive VAWG and counter VAWG preven-tion and response. The entanglement of religion and culture shows how religious ideas can contribute to creating harmful environ-ments for women not only within churches, but in the broader community too. It also highlights that engaging with religion and religious leaders and communities around VAWG prevention and response will always have to take culture into account. Second, we see that Christian communities tend to avoid and/or vilify sex and sexuality. In itself this becomes a harmful practice, but it also directly or indirectly drives other practices harmful to women and girls. Third, churches were revealed as (often) being deeply patri-archal organisations. In this way religious institutions are actually an important pillar upholding the patriarchy. Last, we see how Christian religious experiences can drive VAWG and severely chal-lenge VAWG prevention and response efforts. While this chapter has highlighted key ways in which Christian beliefs, practices, organisation and experiences can lead to VAWG and counter prevention and response efforts, this is not the whole story. Chapter 7 explores how the Christian religion and Christian religious actors can be key allies in ending VAWG and addressing its consequences.

References

Akoko, R.M. and Oben, T.M. (2006). "Christian churches and the democratization conundrum in Cameroon", *Africa Today*, 52(3): 25–48.

Avishai, O. (2008). "'Doing religion'" in a secular world: Women in conservative religions and the question of agency", *Gender and Society*, 22(4): 409–433.

Baker, C. (2012). "Exploring spiritual capital: Resources for an uncertain future?", in M. O'Sullivan and B. Flanagan (eds.), *Spiritual capital: Spirituality in practice in Christian perspective*. Farnham: Ashgate Publishing Limited, 7–22.

Barker, G. (2016). "Male violence or patriarchal violence? Global trends in men and violence", *Sexualidad, Salud y Sociedad (Rio de Janeiro)*, 22: 316–330.

Beyers, J. (2017). "Religion and culture: Revisiting a close relative", *HTS Teologiese Studies/Theological Studies*, 73(1): a3864.

Bradley, T. (2010). "Religion as a bridge between theory and practice in work on violence against women in Rajasthan", *Journal of Gender Studies*, 19(4): 361–375.

El-Damanhoury, I. (2013). "The Jewish and Christian view on female genital mutilation", *African Journal of Urology*, 19(3): 127–129.

Gifford, P. (2008). "Trajectories in African Christianity", *International Journal for the Study of the Christian Church*, 8(4): 275–289.

Greiff, S. (2010). *No justice in justifications: Violence against women in the name of culture, religion, and tradition*. The Global Campaign to Stop Killing and Stoning Women. Viewed from https://documentation.lastradain-ternational.org/doc-center/2446/no-justice-in-justifications-violence-against-women-in-the-name-of-culture-religion-and-tradition [Date accessed: April 6, 2022].

Hunnicutt, G. (2009). "Varieties of patriarchy and violence against women: Resurrecting 'patriarchy' as a theoretical tool", *Violence against Women*, 15(5): 553–573.

Kandiyoti, D. (1988). "Bargaining with patriarchy", *Gender and Society*, 2(3): 274–290.

Kanyoro, M. (2001). "Engendered communal theology: African women's contribution to theology in the twenty-first century", *Feminist Theology*, 9(27): 36–56.

Le Roux, E. (2014). "The role of African Christian churches in dealing with sexual violence against women: The case of the democratic Republic of Congo, Rwanda and Liberia", PhD Dissertation, Stellenbosch University.

Le Roux, E. (2019). "Can religious women choose? Holding the tension between complicity and agency", *African Journal of Gender and Religion*, 25(1): 1–19.

Le Roux, E. (2021). "Jesus is a survivor: Sexual violence and stigma within faith communities", in J.R. Reaves, D. Tombs and R. Figueroa (eds.), *When did we see you naked? Jesus as a victim of sexual abuse.* London: SCM Press, 178–194.

Le Roux, E. and Bartelink, B.E. (2017). *No more 'harmful traditional practices': Working effectively with faith leaders.* Joint Learning Initiative for Faith and Local Communities. Viewed from https://jliflc.com/resources/no-harmful-traditional-practices-working-effectively-faith-leaders/ [Date accessed: September 7, 2022].

Le Roux, E. and Cadavid Valencia, L. (2020). "Partnering with local faith communities: Learning from the response to internal displacement and sexual violence in Colombia", in K. Kraft and O.J. Wilkinson (eds.), *International development and local faith actors: Ideological and cultural encounters.* Oxon: Routledge, 236–250.

Le Roux, E. and Palm, S. (2018). *What lies beneath? Tackling the roots of religious resistance to ending child marriage.* Girls not Brides. Viewed from https://www.girlsnotbrides.org/learning-resources/resource-centre/what-lies-beneath-tackling-the-roots-of-religious-resistance-to-ending-child-marriage-2/ [Date accessed: April 6, 2022].

Le Roux, E. and Palm, S. (2019). *Helping families become non-violent spaces: Exploring the roles of the Anglican Mother' Union in Zambia.* New York, NY: Episcopal Relief and Development.

Link, B.G. and Phelan, J.C. (2001). "Conceptualizing stigma", *Annual Review of Sociology*, 27: 363–385.

Link, B.G. and Phelan, J.C. (2014). "Stigma power", *Social Science and Medicine*, 103: 24–32.

Lovše, N. (2009). "Roles of husbands and wives in the Christian marriage relationship (Ephesians 5)", *KAIROS – Evangelical Journal of Theology*, 3(2): 113–134.

Maluleke, T.S. and Nadar, S. (2002). "Breaking the covenant of violence against women", *Journal of Theology for Southern Africa*, 114: 5–17.

Miller, J.A. (2009). "Wound made fountain: Toward a theology of redemption", *Theological Studies*, 70: 525–554.

Myambo, V. (2018). "Churches as community development locus: Addressing the challenges of the girl child in the Eastern Highlands of Lesotho", Master's Thesis, Stellenbosch University.

Nadar, S. and Potgieter, C. (2010). "Liberated through submission? The worthy woman's conference as a case study of Formenism", *Journal of Feminist Studies in Religion*, 26: 141–151.

Njoh, A.J. and Akiwumi, F.A. (2012). "The impact of religion on women empowerment as a Millenium Development Goal in Africa", *Social Indicators Research*, 107: 1–18.

Palm, S., Le Roux, E. and Bartelink, B.E. (2017). *Christian aid: Case study as part of DFID-funded working effectively with faith leaders to challenge harmful traditional practices.* Joint Learning Initiative for Faith and Local Communities. Viewed from https://www.christianaid.org.uk/sites/default/files/2017-11/Working_effectively_with_faith_leaders_Christian_Aid_case_study_sept_2017.pdf [Date accessed: February 25, 2022].

Para-Mallam, O.J. (2006). "Faith, gender and development agendas in Nigeria: Conflicts, challenges, and opportunities", *Gender and Development*, 14(3): 409–421.

Péclard, D. (1998). "Religion and politics in Angola: The church, the colonial state and the emergence of Angolan nationalism, 1940–1961", *Journal of Religion in Africa*, 28(2): 160–186.

Pfeiffer, J. (2004). "Civil society, NGOs, and the holy spirit in Mozambique", *Human Organization*, 63(3): 359–372.

Ross, K.R. (2004). "Worrisome trends: The voice of the churches in Malawi's third term debate", *African Affairs*, 103(410): 91–107.

Sabar-Friedman, G. (1997). "Church and state in Kenya, 1986–1992: The churches' involvement in the 'game of change'", *African Affairs*, 96(382): 25–52.

Taylor, J. (2005). "Taking spirituality seriously: Northern Uganda and Britain's 'break the silence' campaign", *The Round Table*, 94(382): 559–574.

Uchem, R. (2003). "Overcoming women's subordination in the Igbo African culture and in the Catholic Church", *Critical Half: Annual Journal of Women for Women International*, 1(1): 27–31.

Van Klinken, A.S. (2013). *Transforming masculinities in African Christianity: Gender controversies in times of AIDS.* Farnham, Surrey: Ashgate.

Yang, L.H., Kleinman, A., Link, B.G., Phelan, J.C., Lee, S. and Good, B. (2007). "Culture and stigma: Adding moral experience to stigma theory", *Social Science & Medicine*, 64: 1524–1535.

4

A MUSLIM PERSPECTIVE

Religion as intersecting risk in violence against women and girls

Sandra Iman Pertek

Introduction

> These men take the verse [Qur'an 4:34] literally; they didn't look
> for the meaning behind these letters. My husband is like this. He
> says it is permissible to beat me…When he beats me, I ask, "does
> your religion permit you to do this?" and he says, "yes and that
> Allah made it obligatory for women to obey their husbands", but
> they forget that Allah ordered husbands to be good men and treat
> their women fairly.
>
> (Roqaya from Syria, quoted in Pertek, 2022a:150)

The above comment was shared by Roqaya,[1] a Syrian refugee
woman, I interviewed during data collection in Ankara (Turkey)
in 2019. As a survivor of domestic violence, alongside several other
women, she expressed frustrations about her husband who abused
her, justifying his behaviour based on his religious misbeliefs concerning gender relations in the family.

In this chapter, I discuss violence against women and girls
(VAWG) from a Muslim perspective, drawing upon the voices of 21
Syrian and two Iraqi women survivors and their understanding of

DOI: 10.4324/9781003169086-6

religion. I focus on the influences of Islam on women's experiences of violence, while recognising these often interact with other factors such as gender norms and culture, and so I consider religion as intersecting risk in VAWG. Unlike Chapter 8, where I explore religion as protective resource, here I show ways in which cultural and patriarchally constructed interpretations of religious texts can contribute to women's vulnerability to violence. Findings and discussion are structured alongside Ter Haar's (2011) religious resources: ideas, practices, experience and organisation, as outlined in Chapter 2.

Religious ideas: Ambiguous interpretations and attitudes to violence

Religious beliefs are a foundation of religion, based on and evolving around religious texts and personal experience of religion. What people believe in shapes their worldview, attitudes and behaviours. I begin from exploring what survivors of VAWG believe in and how this can shape their experiences. Muslim religious ideas derive from the primary sources of the Islamic traditions, namely the Qur'an and narrations of the sayings of Prophet Muhammed (PBUH), called the *Sunnah*. Even though Islamic sources condemn violence against women and promote kindness, non-violence in treating women and respecting women, some verses and narrations have been historically interpreted in ambiguous ways, favouring men and justifying certain practices harmful to women and girls. What this looks like in practice may differ over time and place. The relationships between religious worldviews, gender norms and attitudes to VAWG in different religious traditions vary as they are grounded in historical and geographical theologies (Istratii, 2020). Inevitably, religious ideas, as deeply intertwined with social norms, shape VAWG survivors' trajectories.

Religious beliefs often form a framework of reference for believers, shaping their understanding, attitudes and tolerance of VAWG. In this chapter, I specifically refer to one of the most contested and contentious verses of the Qur'an (4:34) – interpretations of which can either cause women to become vulnerable to violence or support their resilience (see Chapter 8). Verse 34 in Chapter 4 (titled *al-nisa*, in English' women') presents a three-stage way that a husband should follow in case of spousal disobedience and lewdness. If (first) admonishing and (second) leaving the conjugal bed does not help make amendments, men are instructed to the last (third) resort of '*idribuhunna*' (traditionally translated as 'disciplining' and 'lightly hitting' and compared to a tap with a toothbrush).

Most refugee women survivors of domestic violence, aged between 18 and 64, whom I met in Turkey, believed that VAWG is not allowed in their religion and the majority of the respondents spoke about the Prophetic practice and faith narratives that counter it. Many respondents' immediate response would be to state "Islam forbids violence against women". Nonetheless, I probed further with 12 women survivors (who each experienced domestic violence) about their understanding of the Qur'anic verse 4:34. They provided different interpretations, with some stating that physical discipline can be appropriate in some circumstances but without harming women. While five of the women felt that hitting a wife is never acceptable based on the Qur'an and *Sunnah*, four stated that gentle hitting can be used as discipline, two felt that hitting is appropriate if a wife makes mistakes and two felt it was allowed if a wife is unfaithful. Yet, although several of these women accepted 'light' violence in situation of *nushuz* (disobedience to husband), they did not apply this exception to the disproportionate violence they had suffered.

Literacy mattered too in shaping tolerance of VAWG. Respondents who felt literate in their religion (i.e. could read the Arabic scripture) could identify the three stages, described in the Qur'an 4:34, which a man should follow in reprimanding a wayward wife and reconcile family conflict. They emphasised that husbands often misinterpreted the third step, using it as an excuse to beat their wives. While some respondents, who identified themselves as unable to read the sacred text, were not aware of varied interpretations of *idribuhunna* and justified abuse, some said that women in general misunderstood the religious text themselves and tolerated abuse in silence:

> And for *idribuhunna*, there's a word before it: advise them, but if they didn't respond, then they can hit them lightly, but in

these times, unfortunately, there are some women who don't listen to their husbands, and some men also take that verse and use it in the wrong way...the women keep silent, they hit them and use *idribuhunna* against their wives and they keep quiet and don't speak, and they didn't know the meaning behind this verse...

(Hanifah from Syria, quoted in Pertek, 2022a:173)

Domestic violence was often tolerated, as several respondents spontaneously called it "a normal thing"; however survivors differed in their understandings of what constitutes misconduct (*nushuz*) deserving a spousal reprimand. According to some, spousal disobedience meant any immoral and anti-religious acts. Survivors who could identify varying interpretations of the Qur'anic verses that relate to disciplining a wife recognised that they themselves are contributing to the continued dominance of patriarchal interpretations of *idribuhunna* and other gendered beliefs, such as accepting polygamy. Indeed, expanding religious knowledge is a continued and contested process, for "religious texts are continuously (re)interpreted" (Khalaf-Elledge, 2021:13). In this process, the social transmission and reproduction of religious teachings can absorb and transmit hegemonic values, shaping women's attitudes to domestic violence. This is why Qur'anic interpretations vary in history, time and place. For instance, Chaudhry (2013) points out that pre-colonial interpretations of the Qur'an were incredibly patriarchal, and although in the postcolonial discourse alternative non-violent interpretations grounded in religious ethics have become available, many Islamic scholars still choose pre-colonial explanations which may help to maintain power disparities. Scholarly interpretations of Qur'an 4:34 illustrate how interpretations can vary. Ammar (2007) introduced four approaches of scholars to interpreting Qur'an 4:34, from (1) permission to discipline one's wife; (2) light and symbolic hitting; (3) interpreting *idribuhunna* as an exception to the wider Islamic principles and taking *idribuhunna* as permissible but not desirable; to (4) interpreting *idribuhunna* as something else than hitting, as per its meaning in other parts of the Qur'an, for example, to 'leave' or to 'separate' (e.g. Hassan, 2013; IICPSR and UNFPA, 2016).

Another religiously (and socially constructed) contested idea which underpins women's subordination is the concept of '*qawamoon*' (Qur'an 4:34), dictating that men should take financial care of their wives. Historically and normatively, *qawamoon* was often interpreted by men (using a patriarchal lens) as permission for men to manage women. However, there are numerous different translations of *qawamoon* in English, including 'manager', 'guardian' and 'maintainer' (Ashrof, 2005). In some communities, *qawamoon* may be interpreted as a dictating that men should rule women in other communities it is interpreted as referring to the responsibility that a man has to provide for his wife's material, financial and emotional needs. What is common, however, to many of these different interpretations is that they may appoint disproportionate decision-making powers to men and marginalise women's position in the family (Hassan, 1995). While some respondents rejected a patriarchal interpretation of the term, others referred to the *qawamoon* to legitimise the unequal power distribution between spouses and their responsibility to obey their husband. For example, Lamia from Syria said: "In our traditions and in the Qur'an also, there is a verse that men have an advantage over women, and from this *Surah*, the women should obey men" (quoted in Pertek, 2022:170). Upon probing Levantine respondents about the institution of *qawamoon*, significant power imbalances came into light, shaped not only by religious beliefs but many other factors, such as previous and concurrent family violence, neglect in childhood, loss of parents and/or poverty.

Similarly, religious interpretations shaped at times behaviours of perpetrators, even if they were described as not religious or not practising. Four survivors, whom I interviewed in Ankara, told me that their husbands used religious beliefs to condone abuse and justify their behaviours, taking advantage of their piety, sarcastically referring to religious text and misusing religious precepts to justify their behaviours. Particularly, as narrated by a handful of domestic violence survivors; women having greater trust in a higher power than their partners could be triggering for abusers to harm them at times. For example, Roqaya from Syria disclosed: "I told him that finding a house is in Allah's hands; if he wants it to be, then it'll be, and he started beating me again, and he scratched my cheeks" (quoted in Pertek, 2022:196). In sum, there was a spectrum of religious interpretations that inform the different ways VAWG is understood by Muslim women. Their ambiguous attitudes operated alongside the continuum of gendered power, simultaneously serving as powerful determinants of resource distribution and gender relations in the household and community.

Religious practices: Violent silencing and (in/direct) harm

I now focus on how religious ideas can generate and enable religiously implicated practices that may deter victims from seeking support and indirectly and directly harm women and girls. What I discuss here are both practices that may be considered as called-for in religious scriptures as well as practices that may be seen as not justified in the scriptures. The latter as socially constructed are likely practices which were developed based on religious (mis) beliefs and wider social norms. One such practice is the notion to keep family matters private with discretion and concealment, which evolved within Muslim ethics, pre-Islamic gender norms and cultural norms of diverse Muslim societies. Keeping private issues private may be motivated by notions of 'modesty' and an understanding of an imagined 'good wife' who can be trusted and who will not expose private matters to strangers. Indeed, a range of religious beliefs dictate that good wives are obedient to their husbands (Qur'an 4:34) and it may be implied that in doing so they endure hardship. Such beliefs can become internalised barriers preventing victims from seeking help. In different geographical locations, the practice of domestic privacy takes on different names. For example, in Senegal it is known as 'Sutura'. A GBV specialist interviewed in my PhD study based on her interactions with survivors described it as follows:

> Sutura is this concept that you must remain private, you know, like you shouldn't disclose everything. You can't talk openly about things you don't like, your wife in public, you

wait until you're in the room, because of the *Sutura*, like this cover…I think that *Sutura* would be translated as discretion… you'd have to go through so much abuse to overcome that *Sutura* barrier…usually they don't tell you, you know, they don't say my husband beat me, or he insults me…they just say 'it's difficult'…

(Lucy, Regional GBV Advisor, International Organisation, Senegal, interview in 2020)

While Lucy indicated that keeping domestic matters private was socially ascribed, the concept links with the archetype of piety promoted in religious communities as a virtue, a licence to prosperous life hereafter and a test of faith and theology in lived experience (Winkler, 2017). Piety of women of faith is a natural and powerful attribute and indeed a form of religious practice. However, abusive environments can build on and misuse piety. Generally, piety is a religious devotion which also commands a duty of maintaining self-respect, manifesting in a series of beliefs and acts related to service to God, which may make survivors endure violence and refrain from help-seeking.

Piety, as a scripturally validated practice, can be misused to justify the perpetration of VAWG and/or continued tolerance of VAWG. In particular, it can be misused to preserve family and individual honour by the concealment of family tensions and domestic abuse based on the assumptions that being an obedient and honourable woman is a prerequisite of piety. Several scriptural verses allude to harnessing honour and respect among women and men. And although the Qur'an calls both women and men to protect their chastity ("…for men and women who guard their chastity… for them has Allah prepared forgiveness and great reward", Qur'an 33:35), cultural norms may focus on women's and girls' chastity as carriers of family honour and purity of lineage. In turn, feminine honour is determined by chastity, over which entire communities and families often feel responsibility for.

Honour and piety are also related concepts, as privacy and piety are. Pious women are seen as honourable women, who ought to protect their reputation. Such expectations can lead survivors to silence themselves to maintain their reputation. Indeed, among the women I met in Turkey, some survivors considered the reporting of violence shameful. They kept silent to maintain their reputation because of wider social norms which blamed survivors for abuse. One woman said: "The problem with the society is that they take victim as it's their fault, it's not the person who is doing that, it's the person who is already a survivor/victim…, it's their fault" (Noor from Syria, quoted in Pertek, 2022:192).

The blaming and silencing of victims meant women rarely sought help. Thus, silencing victims in religious and wider communities becomes violent. Violent silence, shame, blame and honour concerns intertwine and perpetuate VAWG risks. For example, displaced survivors may avoid seeking help because of concerns about dishonour and shame, in addition to fears of losing custody of their children in a foreign land if they disclosed abuse in the household.

> …he told me, "why you came here, what would people say about our honour? That's very shameful, you're a young woman with two children…?"…I stayed with him [a brother of her deceased husband] for one week before my stepbrothers told me that I should go back to Syria or my husband's brother should marry me because many people would talk about family honour, and they told me I should move now or a killing would happen; he'd kill us or we'd kill him.
>
> (Shamila from Syria, quoted in Pertek, 2022a:193)

Dishonouring victims can also become a strategy of perpetrators, as it prevents victims from leaving. In one account of a Syrian survivor in Turkey, her abusive husband aimed to destroy her honour with lies about infidelities and through shaming her publicly. In addition, shame deterred women from seeking support not only concerning domestic violence, but also when they experienced conflict-related sexual violence. Some accounts of women living in conflict-affected settings recalled how powerless victims of violence in war times were due to multiple factors, including religion, as intersecting risk and cross-cutting issue.

> …they [soldiers] were entering homes, if they want, they can take, nobody can stop them, because soldiers with weapons can…they can do anything to you. Women can't speak about that, it is very shameful in our religion and education, in our tradition…Because if you talk you will destroy your future… maybe everyone around you knows your story, nobody will want to marry you…
>
> *(Amira from Syria, quoted in Pertek, 2022a:185)*

Arranged marriage, often enforced to protect family honour, as well as divorce were also religiously implicated practices. In the case of Syrian and Iraqi women, breaking arranged marriages and engagements was considered traditionally unacceptable, culturally inappropriate, shameful and threatening to the family honour, as reported by several Syrian and Iraqi respondents in Turkey. Yasmeen from Syria was one of the women who married as a minor with a considerably older man, whom she divorced years later during her stay in Ankara. She revealed:

> It was an arranged marriage. He came and paid money for my family, and after I met him, I told my mother that I don't want him, and I took the money and gave it back to his family, and my mother said that this is shameful; people will talk about my honour, and that I was engaged to him for 3 months…No, after I met him many times, I decided that I don't want him, but my mother pushed me.
>
> *(interview in 2019)*

Unlike arranged marriages, early and forced marriages are considered impermissible in Islam, as minors are not allowed to enter into binding contracts and so disqualify marriage contract conditions (Pertek and Abdulaziz, 2018). For these reasons, early marriages are also considered as forced marriages. Yet, in efforts to maintain family honour, sometimes early (forced) and arranged marriages are seen as solutions to protect girls' chastity and the family name. Some communities allow minors to marry if they are perceived as physically and socially mature enough, while other communities justify the practice based on orally transmitted tradition of the Prophet Muhammed's marriage with Ayesha bint Abu Bakr, whose specific age of marriage remains unknown and contested. She later became a highly respected figure in Islam – distinguished Islamic scholar and a mother of the believers in the Islamic tradition.

Nevertheless, women and girls subjected to arranged or early and forced marriages may feel unable to withdraw from an arranged marriage and/or to early seek divorce due to the complex intersection between culture, religion and intergenerational gender norms. Religion and culture are inseparable, and mutually constitutive, they may enable and oppose VAWG in local communities. Religion can be a part of a culture by shaping cultural norms, and culture can be a part of religion by shaping religious practices (Ghafournia, 2017). In my study, several Levantine respondents married as minors and endured violence for years due to the cultural expectations of upholding family honour by saving their marriages. For example, for Amira from Syria, divorce was not an option, as her uncle made clear to her his honour-based concerns:

> He said "I came back to Syria after 8 years, because of you. No woman gets divorce in this family...look, you are my brother's daughter, you are my honour, I don't want you to get divorced because this is very bad thing for you..."
>
> *(quoted in Pertek, 2022a:171)*

In addition, some interviewees were encouraged to stay in abusive relationships by family members who were themselves victims of intimate-partner violence, indicating the intergenerational nature of VAWG.

Another phenomenon condoned based on family honour at the intersection of culture and religion was FGM/C which I found in Ethiopia during a gender study in Dekasuftu Woreda. FGM/C in this setting was a common practice to protect girls' chastity and ensure their 'marriageability'. One woman during community awareness activities questioned: "If we stop FGM/C, who [will] marry our girls?" (IRE in Pertek, 2020:143). While FGM/C was perceived as means to protect girls' honour by preventing them from engaging in illicit intimate relationships, girls who had not been cut were stigmatised and ostracised by community members. Women's voices in local communities contended that "FGM/C is our culture; it is difficult to change or stop [it]" (IRE in Pertek, 2020:143). Some of the older women in focus group discussions (above 50 years old) argued that throughout their lives, as Muslims, they believed FGM/C practice was important and allowed. However, during VAWG awareness sessions run by IRE, they had been told that FGM/C is harmful: "I am 57 years old and we were Muslim long time ago; I have never heard before [that] FGM/C is harmful. Why today [has it] become harmful?" (ibid.). Indeed, harmful practices are deeply ingrained in existing social and power structures over time. The above example shows that behaviours may dynamically interact with religious ideas and wider social norms and so faith-sensitive interventions are required to help change mindsets to counter VAWG. I continue the analysis of how the religion–culture–violence nexus was addressed with faith sensitivity in Dekasuftu Woreda in Chapter 8.

Religious experience: Endurance and spiritual violence

Ter Haar (2011) suggests religion may stimulate in believers certain cognitive, psychological and emotional experiences. These experiences can contribute to VAWG and deter healing of victims or counter abuse and facilitate healing (as discussed in Chapter 8). People undergoing religious experiences feel a personal and direct experience of God or God-inspired events, inconceivable to outsiders. Such experiences evoke intense feelings and convictions that can affect all areas of life, including vulnerability and recovery. Religious experiences are often a manifestation of people's religious ideas and practices and can go hand in hand with piety. For example, one survivor residing in Ankara, compared her situation to a *mi'raj* ('the ascension into heaven'), which was the central spiritual experience of the key figure of Islam, Prophet Muhammed (PBUH).

> Sometimes, I talk to Allah and tell him that even the prophets and messengers couldn't handle this life, so how could I handle it?...I remember our prophet's story...His life was very difficult, full of hardships, but regardless of all of that, when he went to "*Sidra Al-Montaha*" [heaven], he preferred to come back to this life to get more reward; that makes me strong. I also read Qur'an, even when I sleep, I see in my dream that I'm reading Qur'an...*Surah* [Chapter] *Al-Waqia*...
>
> (Shamila from Syria, quoted in Pertek, 2022a:238)

While relying on the Prophetic stories instils strength in survivors/ victims, as discussed in detail in Chapter 8, this may also incline them towards inaction and endurance of violence, with feelings of hopelessness and resignation, minimising the importance of this life (Hassouneh-Phillips, 2003). In the above citation, Shamila dreamed about the Qur'anic chapter *Al-Waqia* (in English meaning 'inevitable' or 'the event') which focuses on the afterlife and fates of righteous and unrighteous people. In her case, by questioning how the Prophet could handle the harms of this life, she found respite in holding on to the promise of great reward afterlife (see Chapter 8). However, while facing multiple abuses from different perpetrators, such beliefs became for her a mantra shifting her focus from the present to the future hereafter, playing out as a mixed blessing. While emulating the endurance of the prophets and other key religious figures can be empowering (Haeri, 2007), for some survivors it can minimise their own suffering and deter action. In turn, a psychological relief may hold them back from seeking to change their harmful circumstances.

Similarly, the Islamic virtue of accepting hardship and being grateful to God, whatever the circumstances, may encourage victims to persevere and wait patiently for years – even their whole lives. As such, strength derived from faith can indeed become a palliative measure (Swart, 2013). For example, religious experiences linked to VAWG, underpinned by religious beliefs in destiny and reward in the afterlife, may sometimes delay survivors from help-seeking and lead them to tolerate abuse (Hassouneh-Phillips, 2003). Beliefs in religious incentives can make victims tolerate spousal abuse in hopes of a greater reward, namely the spiritual experience of going to heaven. Such was the case for Mariam from Syria who disclosed: "He swears at us, he gets angry with me, and that's his right, I mean, he's sick, and I totally accept it and endure it; I want to go to heaven..." (quoted in Pertek, 2022:196).

Embodying patience (as a religious virtue) silenced victims, too. For example, some survivors were sometimes advised by religious leaders to remain patient and faithful. For example, Lotifa from Syria said: "He [local imam] would tell me to endure it [her husband's misbehaviour] and be patient when I'd tell him that I am feeling distressed, he'd always tell me to pray and make Duaa [prayer/supplication]" (quoted in Pertek, 2022:174). While the virtue of patience is often preached by religious leaders, it may be misconstrued by victims trapped in abusive relationships. To reduce such risks, faith leaders should link religious teachings on patience with the importance of protecting human life and dignity, as valued religious virtues, too.

Accounting for how religious practices and beliefs shape spiritual experiences can help developing a deeper understanding of survivors' re/actions to VAWG. For example, some survivors, I spoke with, counted on dreams from God to move forward with their lives. Night dreams were interpreted by several survivors as signs from God that gave them courage (see Chapter 8). Another telling example was the religious experience of a pilgrimage – a highly religious moment – during which one victim forgave her husband for protracted abuse and decided to stay with him despite high risks of continued harm. While forgiveness by the victim and the promise of inner transformation by a perpetrator is necessary for healing and family conflict resolution, in practice, it can be a strategy of deterrence furthering a cycle of abuse. Nonetheless, survivors inspired by spiritual experience may believe in their partners' inner transformation. Religious survivors may also pray for perpetrators and believe that the violence will ultimately cease, as several respondents in my study did. Spiritual experiences, expressed in feelings of being guided by religious beliefs, may make victims wait for God to change their situation or until they feel divinely inspired to leave abusive relationships. Indeed, spiritual experiences can inspire passive coping strategies which involve emotional coping methods (Finn, 1985). Several survivors, whom I interviewed in my PhD study, perceived suffering as a sacrifice and a test from God, generating feelings of despair and powerlessness, yet submitting to their destiny. In sum, deeply spiritual experiences may combine with emotions, ultimate reliance on God and a range of religious teachings in ways that lead victims to minimise the harm done to them and delay seeking help.

Finally, spiritual struggles – psychological distress of a religious or spiritual nature – such as feelings of abandonment and punishment by God, can intensify the suffering and hinder the healing of survivors (Rutledge et al., 2021; Pertek, 2022). While there are different causes of spiritual struggles, among others, they can be triggered by spiritual violence as my research found with Syrian and Iraqi women war survivors. Spiritual violence can be broadly described as a misuse of spiritual means to control, harass, demean and exploit others to cause harm. In war conditions, many respondents described how spiritual violence violated their relationship with the divine and infringed on their belief system in ways which challenged their religious experience and caused spiritual struggles. Clearly, violence can work not only on the body but also on the soul by indoctrination of different forms (Galtung, 1969). Reported threat to women's religious beliefs and shrinking freedom of belief was common during religious persecution in Syria, where respondents' beliefs and practices were challenged. Especially some Muslim women felt their religion (Sunni Islam) was compromised when combatants imposed a distorted understanding of religion. In so doing, they inflicted psychological and spiritual violence – in other words – violence on the soul of religious women, by violating their relationships with the divine and altering their religious experience. One woman said:

> I lived with Daesh for five months. They wanted to make us go backward, to the era of ignorance. If a strange man comes to your area, you should cover your face and hands, and if you

walk with your husband with your face uncovered, they will stone your husband. I felt so scared, we arrived at a situation where we were thinking, "Is that Islam?". We started questioning our faith and many people stopped believing in it. They would find mistakes in everything we do, our prayers, the way we recite Shahada [the testimony of faith]...But our religion is not like that.

(Amina from Syria, quoted in Pertek, 2022a:184)

Drawing upon Galtung's (1990) concept of de-socialisation (e.g. moving away from one's culture and being resocialised into another) as a form of direct violence, I argue that distorting and violating certain religious experiences and imposing others can be considered as a form of violence. In addition, women survivors of war, I interviewed in Turkey, spoke about distrusting faith groups and religious organisations, having experienced severe violations of freedom of religion during the conflict in Syria. Such aversion was underpinned by their experiences of religious persecution and inter-sectarian discrimination. These women preferred to rely on their own understanding of religion and direct connection with God to avoid oppressive interpretations. They also developed mistrust towards religious leaders and preferred to rely on their own religious knowledge drawing on their spiritual capital.

Religious organisation: Dictating patriarchal (dis)order

In this section, I finally look at religious organisation to explore how power imbalances in religious communities can constitute (dis)order normalising VAWG. Violence, in turn, can constitute order (Jakobsen, 2016). I explore the gender-culture and religion nexus with impacts on and of VAWG in religious organisation/ communities, showing how religious ideas, practices and experiences manifest and interact in lived experiences of religious communities.

Religion offers a system of values and symbols with emotional impact, altruistic commitments and community through shared rituals and beliefs (Turner, 1991). Yet, religion does not have agency; as it does not do anything on its own (Beckford, 2003), these are religious organisation, communities and individuals that bring religion to life. A process of enacting the religion is gendered and so are the structures of religious communities that are formed as a result. Patriarchy influences the ways religion is enacted and embodied by religious communities, often twisting religious interpretations which may advantage some and disadvantage others in producing hierarchical gender relations. Patriarchy literally means 'rule of a father' and was first deployed by feminist discourse post-1960s to systematically analyse men's superiority and women's subordination. It refers to a set of ideas that justify male domination and create gender disparities in power across cultures (Ahmad et al., 2004), including in religious community structures. Patriarchy dominates within both religion and culture shaping a patriarchal (dis)order where men may play dominant role in public sphere, and women may be expected to play subordinate role. Religious beliefs sometimes are (mis)used to justify such order of existence and can "confine women to traditional roles" (Ferris, 2011:623). For instance, despite the fact that over half of Islamic religious sources were narrated by women (most by Ayesha, Prophet Muhammed's wife), certain exegeses are used to block female leadership by seizing power and neglecting women's views.

An example of patriarchal (dis)order in religious organisation was vividly illustrated by refugee women I met in Turkey. They explained that patriarchal attitudes and behaviours in some Muslim communities were driven by a lack of religious knowledge and individual piety among men. The women argued that, in general, men in their community did not know how to follow the Prophetic tradition of kindness and honouring women. Instead, they viewed women as incomplete in their religious duties (as they are not required to pray and fast during menses) and men as intellectually superior because of women's presumed faith 'deficiencies'. One woman explained:

> There is another Hadith that says women's minds aren't complete, and their religion isn't complete, but it's because we

have our periods and we don't pray nor fast during this time so our religion is not complete from that side, they [men] know all of this but they don't understand.

(Samira from Syria, interview in 2019)

Beliefs belittling women are in opposition to the Islamic thought that states that God created all human beings perfectly regardless of their gender (Qur'an, 95:4). Yet, the perceived "incompleteness" in religious duties during women's menses spilled over into other areas of life, for instance, as reported by several respondents, exclusion from important family decisions, such as naming of children. Several women reflected on the selective uptake of religion by men in their communities and felt that men should increase their religious knowledge by learning from their role model, Prophet Muhammed, about how to treat women and girls appropriately.

The most thing we need as Arabs is spreading awareness and educating men about women's rights here in Turkey because most of them need a psychological cure to their minds…They need to know their religion better…Allah said that they should be soft with the women, but men in our community only care about that verse that allows marrying more than once. That's what they understand from the Qur'an and from the religion. They didn't look at how the Prophet was treating his wives and daughters; they don't care about that, and because of that, we need good Imams in our religion.

(Mira from Syria, interview in 2019)

Refugee women in Turkey reported different causes of family violence which were related to the structures of their communities. The key reasons cited for normalising VAWG, indirectly intersected with religious beliefs and included patriarchal cultural and tribal gender norms, such as male dominance and female subordination, pressure on women to maintain family honour and remain obedient to her husband and her mother-in-law as well as family pressure on men to discipline their wives. Survivors spoke of a culture of tolerating the physical punishment of women, in which members of religious communities rarely intervened as abuse was justified intergenerationally. Women of previous generations endured violence too, normalising these behaviours. Such finding is supported by a survey by UN Women on masculinity norms in MENA which found that only a minority of Muslim men rejected the statement that religion can be used to justify violence against women (El Feki et al., 2017).

A similar phenomenon of gender injustice was apparent in the Somali Regional State. In the focus group discussions in a gender study with the Somali community in remote areas of Dekasuftu Woreda[2] in 2015, I identified that both women and men valued their gender roles differently. Foremost, men and women saw men's position in front of God as superior to women. In support of such claim both women and men respondents spoke about the story of creation and Eve's origin from Adam's rib, which may allude to Christian tradition. The narration of Eve's creation from Adam's rib is considered in some Muslim religious sources as inauthentic (Hassan, 1995; Ashrof, 2005). And although religious communities showed some awareness of the equality of souls regardless of one's gender (as created from a single soul, Qur'an 7:189), this did not translate into attributing equal societal value to women and men in real life which as a result manifested in varying forms of violence discussed herein. Local men generally considered themselves as more important contributors to socio-economic life and as the rightful decision-makers in the family. Local women did not criticise this gendered order, as it had appeared to them as natural "conditions of existence" (Bourdieu, 1977:167). Most had been socialised into believing that being a 'good wife' might equate with fulfilling their religious duty of obedience. Both men and women attached male leadership in the household to a divine order, which was believed to be prescribed in the religious scriptures. Even if a husband did not provide financially for his wife, he was still often considered a legitimate head of household.

In Dekasuftu Woreda, FGM/C, early marriage and domestic violence were identified as highly tolerated practices by both women and men. The tolerance of women's subordination was also widespread and normalised from an early age. Girls, I interviewed in schools, told me that overall their peers attended school until they got married or dropped out due to domestic duties such as fetching water and caring for siblings. Some girls who attended madrassas spoke about being taught the socio-religious etiquette of being a woman, including what to do and not do during their menses and maintaining a religious attire, yet they were not taught women's rights in the Islamic tradition. Similarly, girls' and women's rights were not discussed in public in their religious communities, perhaps perpetuating religious illiteracy on women's position in society. During my visit, when I asked women about notions of equality, most were opposed to what they considered the Western concept of gender equality, seeing it as incompatible with their lifestyle as mothers. Although motherhood is highly esteemed in Islam and believers are obliged to respect mothers, the way women were often treated by male relatives did not reflect such commitments.

Patriarchal gender norms are known to lead to abuse of power and violence in family and community. One of the commonly reported protection concerns by participants in community conversations was domestic violence in the home, which was seen as a measure to discipline a wife, widely tolerated in local communities of Dekasuftu Woreda. One man illustrated such abusive and discriminatory attitudes:

> Woman should [be] beaten because they are like children and therefore need to be punished [physically] when they make mistakes...sometimes women need to be beaten even when they are depressed to stimulate them...beating is the solution for women to discipline them. Otherwise, the women undermine the husbands up to the point that it will be difficult to identify who is the husband or the wife.
>
> *(Kale, a male representative from the Sero Kebele,[3]*
> *IRE quoted in Pertek, 2020:142)*

In these communities, domestic violence was seen as 'good beating' (coined by Jakobsen, 2015), as it helped maintain power and differentiated gender roles between spouses to uphold distribution of labour and community structures. While participants did not cite religious reasons to justify domestic violence, the intertwinement of culture and tradition appeared to shape gender norms in these communities. Similarly, in the same communities, women condoned VAWG too, reflecting how religious communities were socialised and structured. For example, some women submitted to social norms tolerating violence. Some believed acts of spousal violence symbolised marital love from their concerned husbands. Equally, some women perceived that a lack of violence in marriage signalled a problem in marriage. One respondent said:

> I believe being beaten by [my] husband is right and acceptable … if [my] husband did not beat [me] when [I] make a mistake it implies that there is something wrong with marriage or [my] husband doesn't love [me].
>
> *(Sahra, a female representative from Kudabul Kebele, IRE quoted in Pertek, 2020:142)*

Concurrently, the justifications of domestic abuses dominantly conflated with traditional beliefs in spiritual possessions of unrighteous wives among religious communities. Use of force was justified by some men in Dekasuftu Woreda as a measure to verify a woman's spiritual purity. Some newly married men used to hit their brides on the first night of their union to identify if a bride is controlled by evil spirits. If a woman submitted to violence, she was deemed chase and clean from spirits, while resistance indicated spirit possession. A woman accused of evil possession would be tied to a tree and forced into cleansing procedure (Pertek, 2020). In addition, marriage by inheritance was common, although not linked with religious beliefs but rather culture. Many widows believed that marrying a brother of her deceased husband was not just a cultural but also a religious practice obligatory upon a widow. Some women believed they would risk losing their children and property if they refused to marry a relative of their deceased husband, or had they re-married outside of the deceased husband's family they would be required to pay compensation, that is, ten camels or the equivalent (Pertek, 2020). Some women feared that they would lose a chance to remarry at all.

The above examples demonstrate how patriarchal gender and cultural norms, often intersecting with but also going beyond religious ideas, practices and experiences, intertwine and manifest in religious communities. The culture–religion–abuse nexus requires the analysis from "within the Muslim cultural context" as historical and geographic locations affect cultures (McKerl, 2009:2001). Religious communities are the outcome constituted by, and constitutive of, social relations with power relations (Winter, 2006). Social norms, as part of culture, are rather inseparable from religion. Faith-based gender 'schemas' and 'ideals', which prove religious, and social norms enacted by religious communities are inseparable (Manji, 2018:212). Interactions between religion and culture vary over place and time, "…as a cultural aspect the interpretation and expression of religions will also be contextually constructed and under constant change" (Askeland and Dohlie, 2015:263). Similarly, religious communities constantly evolve alongside changing religious manifestations and so intersecting risks to violence.

Conclusions

Religion can operate as an intersecting risk to VAWG, often in interaction with other factors such as gender norms, culture and patriarchy. Different religious resources can contribute to experiences of violence. Patriarchal interpretations, readings of religious texts out of context, varying understandings of religion and different levels of religious literacy of survivors and perpetrators may lead to power imbalances and tolerance of abuse. In this chapter, in particular, I examined how interpretations of the contentious verse of the Qur'an (4:34) can affect women's vulnerability to gendered harm. I looked at how religiously implicated practices around honour and piety can silence survivors and directly and indirectly perpetrate abuse. I also outlined how religious experiences can encourage survivors to endure/submit to violence and cause spiritual tensions, pointing to the necessity for research, policy and practice to better understand the link between religious experiences and VAWG. Finally, I explored how religious communities may organise themselves in ways dictating patriarchal (dis)order, focusing on the challenges in religious communities. I looked at how the religious beliefs, practices and experiences can interact together in shaping structures, gender norms and behaviours, often in ways undermining women's safety and exacerbating vulnerability to violence. I problematised the deeply intricated religion and culture nexus drawing upon the programmatic experience from Dekasuftu Woreda in Ethiopia's Somali Regional Estate, which I further explore in Chapter 8, highlighting the need for policy and practice to attend to these complex intertwinements. In sum, religious and cultural expressions across two contexts created a compound of different beliefs and practices, shaping experiences of VAWG. The solutions for rupturing violence and positive change are likely to come from within, drawing upon the individual and communal resources of survivors and religious communities.

Notes

1 All names of respondents are pseudonymized.
2 A *Woreda* is an administrative district in Ethiopia.
3 A *Kebele* is the smallest administrative unit of Ethiopia, similar to a ward or a neighbourhood.

References

Ahmad, F., Riaz, S., Barata, P. and Stewart, D.E. (2004). "Patriarchal beliefs and perceptions of abuse among South Asian immigrant women", *Violence Against Women*, 10(3): 262–282. doi:10.1177/1077801203256000.

Ammar, N.H. (2007). "Wife battery in Islam: A comprehensive understanding of interpretations", *Violence Against Women*, 13(5): 516–526. doi:10.1177/1077801207300658.

Ashrof, V.A.M. (2005). *Islam and gender justice*. Delhi: Kalpaz Publications.

Askeland, G.A. and Døhlie, E. (2015). "Contextualizing international social work: Religion as a relevant factor", *International Social Work*, 58(2): 261–269. doi:10.1177/0020872813482958.

Beckford, J.A. (2003). *Social theory and religion*. Cambridge: Cambridge University Press. doi:10.1017/CBO9780511520754.

Bourdieu, P. (1977). *Outline of a theory of practice*. Cambridge Studies in Social and Cultural Anthropology. Cambridge: Cambridge University Press. doi:10.1017/CBO9780511812507.

Chaudhry, A.S. (2013). *Domestic violence and the Islamic tradition*. Oxford: Oxford University Press.

El Feki, S., Heilman, B. and Barker, G. (2017). "Understanding masculinities: Results from the international men and gender equality survey in the middle east and north Africa", UN Women.

Ferris, E. (2011). "Faith and humanitarianism: It's complicated", *Journal of Refugee Studies*, 24(3): 606–625. doi:10.1093/jrs/fer028.

Finn, J. (1985). "The stresses and coping behaviour of battered women", *Social Casework*, 66(6): 341–349.

Galtung, J. (1969). "Violence, peace, and peace research", *Journal of Peace Research*, 6(3): 167–191. Viewed from https://www.jstor.org/stable/422690 [Date accessed: June 30, 2021].

Galtung, J. (1990). "Cultural violence", *Journal of Peace Research*, 27(3): 291–305. doi:10.1177/0022343390027003005.

Ghafournia, N. (2017). "Muslim women and domestic violence: Developing a framework for social work practice", *Journal of Religion & Spirituality in Social Work: Social Thought*, 36(1–2): 146–163. doi:10.1080/15426432.2017.1313150.

Haeri, D.S. (2007). "Resilience and post-traumatic recovery in cultural and political context", *Journal of Aggression, Maltreatment & Trauma*, 14(1–2): 287–304. doi:10.1300/J146v14n01_15.

Hassan, R. (1995). "The development of feminist theology as a means of combating injustice toward women in Muslim communities/culture", *European Judaism: A Journal for the New Europe*, 28(2): 80–90.

Hassouneh-Phillips, D. (2003). "Strength and vulnerability: Spirituality in abused American Muslim women's lives", *Issues in Mental Health Nursing*, 24(6–7): 681–694. doi:10.1080/01612840305324.

IICPSR and UNFPA (2016). *Islamic perspectives on gender-based violence*. Cairo: International Islamic Center for Population Studies and Research at Al-Azhar University (IICPSR) and United Nations Population Fund (UNFPA).

Istratii, R. (2020). *Adapting gender and development to local religious contexts: A decolonial approach to domestic violence in Ethiopia*. Abingdon: Routledge.

Jakobsen, H. (2015). "The good beating. Social norms supporting men's partner violence in Tanzania", PhD Dissertation, University of Bergen.

Jakobsen, H. (2016). "How violence constitutes order: Consent, coercion, and censure in Tanzania", *Violence Against Women*, 24(1): 45–65. doi:10.1177/1077801216678091.

Khalaf-Elledge, N. (2021). Scoping study: Looking back to look forward. The role of religious actors in gender equality since the Beijing Declaration. Washington DC: Joint Learning Initiative on Faith and Local Communities.

Manji, K. (2018). "Articulating the role of social norms in sustaining intimate partner violence in Mwanza, Tanzania", PhD Dissertation, London School of Hygiene and Tropical Medicine.

McKerl, A. (2009). "Gender, multiculturalism and violence: Developing intersectional methodologies from a Muslim point of view", PhD Thesis, University of Aberdeen.

Pertek, S.I. (2020). "Deconstructing Islamic perspectives on sexual and gender-based violence, toward a faith inclusive approach", in A.A. Khan and A. Cheema (eds.), *Islam and International Development: Insights for working with Muslim communities.* Rugby: Practical Action Publishing, 131–152.

Pertek, S. (2022a). "Religion, forced migration and the continuum of violence: an intersectional and ecological analysis", PhD Dissertation, University of Birmingham.

Pertek, S.I. (2022b). "'God helped us': Resilience, religion and experiences of gender-based violence and trafficking among African forced migrant women", *Social Sciences*, 11(5): 201. doi:10.3390/socsci11050201.

Pertek, S.I. and Abdulaziz, S. (2018). *Don't force me: A policy brief on early and forced marriage.* Birmingham: Islamic Relief Worldwide.

Rutledge, K., Pertek, S., Abo-Hilal, M. and Fitzgibbon, A. (2021). "Faith and mental health and psycho-social support among displaced Muslim women", *Forced Migration Review*, 66.

Swart, E. (2013). "Doing survival: Strategies for coping with gender-based violence in Kenya's Kibera Slum", *Affilia*, 28(1): 40–50. doi:10.1177/0886109912470111.

Ter Haar, G. (2011). "Religion and development: Introducing a new debate", in G. ter Haar (ed.), *Religion and development: Ways of transforming the world.* London: Hurst Publishers, 3–25.

Turner, B.S. (1991). *Religion and social theory.* London: SAGE Publications Ltd.

Winkler, K. (2017). "Reflecting on European migration and refugees: From a feminist perspective", *Journalism and Mass Communication*, 7(2). doi:10.17265/2160-6579/2017.02.003.

Winter, B. (2006). "Religion, culture and women's human rights: Some general political and theoretical considerations", *Women's Studies International Forum*, 29(4): 381–393. doi:10.1016/j.wsif.2006.05.004.

5

JOINT REFLECTIONS ON RELIGION CONTRIBUTING TO VIOLENCE AGAINST WOMEN AND GIRLS

Sandra Iman Pertek and Elisabet le Roux

In the preceding two chapters, we discussed how Christianity and Islam can adversely contribute to violence against women and girls (VAWG) perpetration, vulnerability and victimhood. Drawing upon the authors' findings, evidence from research and analysis of relevant literature in different countries, the chapters shed light on the negative impacts of religion on experiences of VAWG. Here we offer joint reflections on how religion becomes practically implicated in VAWG and what this means for VAWG policy and practice.

First and foremost, we observe that both religions, influenced by patriarchy, can contribute to VAWG. Gender norms, as a root cause of gendered violence, are often maintained and mediated by religious ideas, expressed as faith-based gender 'schemas' and 'ideals' (Manji, 2018:212). Clearly, then, transforming gender norms will, in such settings, require engaging with religion. Yet, illustrated in both empirical chapters, culture and religion are deeply entangled and mutually co-constitutive. Social and cultural norms and practices blend and merge with religion. Efforts to disentangle culture and religion may be counter-productive against the reality of how deeply emmeshed religion and culture are. For example, in some

DOI: 10.4324/9781003169086-7

communities certain practices such as FGM/C or early marriage may be perceived as religious and as cultural practices in other communities. Numerous interpretations of religious texts (Bible and Qur'an) across time, communities and geographical locations show us how deeply religion and culture are intertwined.

In Le Roux's Chapter 3, we see early marriage as associated with religious practices, while some practices may have no religious justification but manifest cultural expressions, as in the case of marriage by inheritance and honour-based violence, as discussed in Pertek's Chapter 4. Therefore, we suggest that VAWG prevention and response embrace a mixed reality and develop tools to deconstruct these multiple layers of the conditions around which religion manifests. As various practices can mix cultural and religious justifications, initiatives to delink harmful practices from religions, as in the case of female genital mutilation and/or cutting (FGM/C) (discussed in Chapter 4), are essential to mitigate harm efficiently. In practice, the engagement with religion to end VAWG needs to undertake an intersectional approach and develop faith-sensitive tools that could recognise how religion interacts with other factors, such as culture and gender norms, in shaping VAWG experiences, and help reflect these lived experiences in 'ending VAWG' programmes. For example, developing intersectional analysis tools accounting for the role of religion in VAWG would be important (Pertek, 2022).

As both chapters also help us learn more about the entanglement between culture and religion, in our reflections we consider what this means for VAWG prevention and response. We hope that our reflections help inform what VAWG programming in faith settings could look like. We highlight the need to explore the religious, cultural and gendered expressions and understandings of religions in local communities. Practitioners should engage with cultural understandings of religion and misused verses of the scriptures when working with faith communities on VAWG. Thus, we suggest that religious literacy and gender sensitivity among practitioners and policymakers are essential competencies to engage with the most frequently cited controversial interpretations of religious texts and practices that often underpin VAWG in religious settings. Developing gendered religious literacy can help increase awareness of gendered issues in local religions and challenge stigmatisation of the interactions between religion and VAWG. In doing so, engaging with the insiders of faith communities can facilitate access to local guidance enabling adequate contextualisation of interventions, as discussed by Le Roux in Chapter 3.

Second, currently male-dominated interpretations of sacred texts continue to dominate mainstream understanding in communities, and egalitarian perspectives are rare. Patriarchal systems of religions have direct and indirect influences on VAWG perpetration. Patriarchy impacts religious views through permeating and twisting religious interpretations – as shown by Le Roux in discussion on religious organisations and by Pertek on religious communities. We need to go beyond simply blaming patriarchy to developing approaches that deconstruct and address the patriarchal influences in religion. Such approaches will allow us to challenge the status quo, recognising the diverse factors underpinning patriarchy and gender inequalities. One of the key factors upholding patriarchy is imbalance of power. To help balance power in faith communities, initiatives aiming to dismantle religious misconceptions and harness egalitarian teachings in faith spaces can be a source of transformation for some communities.

Third, reflecting on the last two chapters, we discern that religious beliefs can hinder and impede engagement with the sensitive topics and taboos related to VAWG in religious communities. Le Roux's Chapter 3, in discussing the sex taboo, illustrates how hegemonic views within churches dominate and dictate how sex is perceived, vilifying sexuality, establishing men as in control and encouraging wifely submission. Such attitudes can lead to coercive sex within marriages, often stemming from the lack of awareness of the sexual religious ethics present across different religious traditions. Sexual religious ethics do not condone coercive marital relationships but rather encourage healthy and safe intimacy. In faith communities, sex is mostly not seen as a religious matter. When it is discussed, it is usually in relation to the control of sexuality, focusing on topics such as virginity, chastity and fidelity. Viewing sexuality as taboo has real-life impacts on VAWG programming, reducing entry points for prevention of intimate-partner and non-partner sexual violence, and requires extensive groundwork to sensitise communities to tackle these violations from within.

Moreover, we observe that faith communities silence victims with religious practices and experiences, directly and indirectly, and in the process normalise abuse. For example, certain narratives in faith communities encourage victims to keep family secrets and stay in abusive relationships, while the imagined protection of family honour through defending women's chastity and reputation can violate women's freedoms and autonomy. Religious ideas and beliefs, alongside social and cultural norms and knowledge systems, shape attitudes to VAWG that may delay help-seeking or even lead to the perpetration of VAWG, as was illustrated in Pertek's chapter with FGM/C and domestic violence in the Dekasuftu Woreda. Divorce is not desirable and often stigmatised. Survivors are expected to forgive perpetrators, change their own behaviours and be good wives. Women's sacrifice in marriage, through enduring abuse silently, can be compared with religious martyrdom, in which victims expect a reward for their suffering hereafter. Perpetrators can use a range of religious beliefs to sustain the cycle of violence.

We also see that faith communities and religious organisations can embody gender imbalances in their structures and certain practices, such as stigmatising survivors, encouraging endurance of abuse and male-dominated leadership, which can seem strategic in upholding social order. Faith spaces can often exclude women from decision-making and make survivors of VAWG feel unsafe and condemned. Faith organisations and communities, as they overwhelmingly remain patriarchal institutions, can reinforce the status quo and men's domination to maintain their power, inadvertently perpetuating patriarchy. Yet they also have an ability to challenge injustice, as we discuss in Chapters 7 and 8. Therefore, efforts to work with religion to address VAWG need to engage with religious structures to help promote women's participation and support a balance shift.

Furthermore, the two empirical chapters illustrate the importance of accounting for religious experiences, such as revelations, dreams, visions and miracles. These can play an important role in the lives of believers and should not be dismissed, for they can affect the cognition and emotions of both survivors and perpetrators. We noted that in both religions, religious experiences could create spiritual struggles and tensions, for example, around beliefs in redemption, patience, being tested by God, emulating Prophets and other key figures who faced hardships in their lives, often leading victims to minimise their own suffering. Religious experiences may therefore be a part of the 'religious toolkit' that keep women trapped in abusive relationships. Examples of different religious experiences, as discussed in the preceding chapters, show they can help women justify violence and draw strength to endure violence, hindering these women from actually leaving violent situations.

In addition, our empirical chapters highlight the importance of working with women survivors around shame and self-blame to help them to rupture the cycle of violence and transform their feelings of powerlessness. As we noted, women survivors who are religious may tend to rely on religion, as a palliative measure, which can help them to endure abuse and avoid change. This may be counter-productive, as it delays help-seeking. Proactive, religiously inspired tactics are needed to help survivors move on with their lives safely from harmful relationships. Women's empowerment programmes need to raise awareness about VAWG in religious spaces, too. Furthermore, drawing upon female role models featured in religious traditions can help to inspire ambition, confidence and faith-informed resistance to VAWG among religious survivors.

We also see that ambiguous and subjective interpretations of religious texts can shape the vulnerability of women and girls to abuse. Both Christianity and Islam are monotheistic religions, although there are theological overlaps and differences. However, the ways in which the scriptures may be (mis)used by survivors and perpetrators to justify VAWG are similar, with the selective use of texts which constantly evolve in the process of interpretation (Askeland and Døhlie, 2015). Verses of the Bible and Qur'an can be misused or taken out of context, while alternative interpretations or forgotten apocryphal texts (narrated by women) are ignored. Even when religious texts are originally narrated, as heard from Prophet Muhammed, and reported by learned women across centuries (Nadwi, 2013), women's authority can still be undermined. This is the case in Islam, where over half of the religious sources (hadiths) are narrated by women, especially Ayesha bint Abu-Bakr – yet patriarchal readings and interpretations continue to dominate in religious communities.

Finally, both preceding chapters emphasise that religion and gender are socially constructed, embodied and enacted by social actors. Religious constructs that drive VAWG are diverse and located in a social context. Although religion may carry different meanings for different people, it commonly affects people's thinking, feelings and behaviours. Yet, religion carries substance and material basis of religious faith, which may be unknown to outsiders. These transcendent notions of religion intertwined with religious experiences play a meaningful role in shaping the lived realities of survivors of both religions. Such religious influences should be reflected in interventions aimed at responding to their needs.

References

Askeland, G.A. and Døhlie, E. (2015). "Contextualizing international social work: Religion as a relevant factor", *International Social Work*, 58(2): 261–269. doi:10.1177/0020872813482958.

Manji, K. (2018). "Articulating the role of social norms in sustaining intimate partner violence in Mwanza, Tanzania", PhD Dissertation, London School of Hygiene and Tropical Medicine. doi:10.17037/PUBS.04647114.

Nadwi, M.A. (2013). *Al-Muhaddithat: The women scholars in Islam*. 2nd revised edition. Oxford: Interface Publications Ltd.

PART III

Religion countering violence against women and girls

6

ORIENTATION

The role of religion in countering violence against women and girls

Elisabet le Roux and Sandra Iman Pertek

In Part III we explore how religion can play a role in addressing violence against women and girls (VAWG). Two chapters, one focused on Christian settings and one focused on Muslim communities, draw on empirical work conducted by the authors to unpack the positive roles that religion can play in countering VAWG and supporting survivors. Part III concludes with a reflection chapter (Chapter 9).

Conceptual framework: Religious resources in countering VAWG

As motivated in the Introduction, Gerrie ter Haar's four categories of religious resources are used as conceptual framework for organising the discussion in the two empirical chapters in this section focusing on how religion counters VAWG.

Religious ideas can counter VAWG in different ways. The content of people's religious beliefs can directly oppose VAWG (e.g. categorically state that it is wrong), can promote principles that counter VAWG (e.g. gender equality, non-violence and sanctity of

DOI: 10.4324/9781003169086-9

all human life) or can be interpreted/leveraged in opposition to VAWG (e.g. love, respect and charity). Religious ideas can also be the driver behind VAWG response, translating into practical and spiritual support for survivors (Beaman-Hall and Nason-Clark, 1997). Furthermore, religious ideas can motivate and strengthen believers to actively resist and oppose VAWG. For example, Raising Voices and Trócaire developed SASA! Faith, an initiative in which leaders, members and believers of a faith come together to prevent VAWG and HIV. At the core of its approach to ending VAWG, it inspires everyone to live the faith-based values of justice, peace and dignity in their intimate-partner relationships (Raising Voices, 2016). Sisters in Islam, a non-governmental organisation in Malaysia, uses the same approach by claiming the rights of Muslim women by using Islam as a frame of reference, identifying and promoting Islamic ideas that support equality and justice (Basarudin, 2016). In our chapters' exploration of how religious ideas counter VAWG, we unpack what people actually believe and why and how it drives opposition to VAWG and its consequences.

Religious practices refer to the way people behave based on their religious beliefs. These religious practices can directly oppose VAWG or be leveraged as part of opposition or resistance to VAWG. For example, the religious practices of reading scripture and saying prayers can help survivors leave violent relationships and overcome the trauma they have experienced. Bradley (2010), in studying violence against women in Rajasthan, found women using religious ritual as a source of strength and courage in responding to violence. The practice of seeking counselling from religious leaders has the potential to ensure that those experiencing unhealthy relationships and/or violence receive the support that they need. Chalfant et al. (1990) argue that this is as counselling by religious leaders "has something different to offer in terms of (the) spiritual resources undergirding this type of counselling" (Chalfant et al., 1990:310).

People form communal structures with fellow believers, and such **religious organisation** can be an important resource in addressing VAWG. The structure of the religious organisation (e.g. the leaders, the different sub-groups formed, such as women's groups and youth groups) can be leveraged in VAWG prevention and response. Religious leaders, for example, have status, normative authority and power to influence people's attitudes and behaviours around issues such as intimate-partner violence, sexuality, FGM/C, child marriage, rape and family dishonour (Tomkins et al., 2015). The religious organisation as a whole (e.g. a faith-based organisation) can also be instrumental in addressing VAWG. For example, the Baptist Community in Central Africa (a Christian church) in the eastern DRC runs approximately 10% of all the faith-based schools in the region and decided to launch an intervention to address sexual violence in schools. It trained staff members on how to use the Bible to initiate discussions on power, justice and steps to address sexual violence (Beasley et al., 2010).

Finally, **religious experiences** can form a crucial part of addressing VAWG, especially when it comes to VAWG response and the healing journey of survivors. Prayers, dreams, visions and spiritual experiences, while often an ignored resource in formal VAWG response interventions, can form an important part of a survivor's recovery. These experiences can play a central role in helping survivors from only coping for survival, to resilient self-efficacy and healing (Drumm et al., 2014). In their study of 42 survivors of intimate-partner violence, Drumm et al. ascribed these survivors' resilience dynamics to a "personal, individual understanding of and inner connection to a transcendent higher power God, or even more broadly to a 'search for the sacred', rather than to a identification with or relationship to a religious system" (Drumm et al., 2014:391). The value of religious experiences for survivors should not be underestimated. For example, Bowland et al. (2012) found that participants in group psychotherapy that discussed spiritual struggles related to abuse and developed spiritual coping resources had significantly lower depressive symptoms, anxiety and physical symptoms than the control group.

Overview of Part III

In writing Chapter 7 ("A Christian perspective: Drawing on religion to prevent and respond to VAWG"), Le Roux engaged in an inductive analysis process with data from 14 different studies she was part of over the past 12 years. However, Chapter 7 relies on extensive examples and illustrations from only four of these studies. The background, aim and methodology of two of these studies (the 2018–2019 study of the Anglican Mothers' Union in Zambia and violence against women and children [Le Roux and Palm, 2019] and the 2010 study on the role of African Christian churches in addressing sexual violence against women in conflict-affected settings, conducted in the Democratic Republic of Congo, Rwanda and Liberia [Le Roux, 2010, 2014]) were already discussed in Chapter 2. Therefore, more background and methodological details are offered below of only the two studies that were not introduced in Chapter 2.

In 2015, Tearfund and HEAL Africa started implementing a three-year VAWG intervention funded by UK Aid from the UK government under the *What Works to Prevent Violence Against Women and Girls?* Global Programme. The aim of the intervention was to mobilise, train and equip religious leaders to become catalysts within their own communities in order to address the underlying root causes of VAWG from a faith perspective. Implemented in 15 villages in Ituri province in the DRC, the intervention trained, mentored and supported 75 religious leaders (Christian and Muslim) and 30 gender champions (community leaders with a willingness to address gender-related matters; almost always also belonging to a church or mosque) to address harmful attitudes, behaviours and social norms that drive gender inequality and VAWG. Both qualitative research (a panel study) and quantitative research (baseline and endline community surveys) accompanied the intervention. Le Roux was part of the team responsible for the research. The panel study (a qualitative, longitudinal study in which data is collected from the same sample at several points in time) consisted of four panel visits at approximately eight-month intervals and was conducted with ethical clearance from Stellenbosch University's Research Ethics Committee: Humanities. The panel visits started in July 2015, with the last one conducted in August 2017 (Le Roux, 2018) and a thematic analysis of qualitative data conducted. The baseline community survey sample comprised 751 respondents, and at endline 1,198 respondents, all from randomly selected households in the 15 villages (Le Roux et al., 2020).

Channels of Hope (CoH) is one of the key methodologies used by World Vision for mobilising religious leaders and local religious communities to respond to the core issues affecting their communities. CoH Gender was developed in 2008, with the gender 'flavour' helping participants explore gender and VAWG through using the Bible. In October 2013, World Vision started a five-year, externally funded project entitled 'Channels of Hope Gender Scale Up Project', targeting 18 different countries. In 2019, Le Roux was asked to conduct an external evaluation of the Scale Up Project. The study was qualitative and a thematic analysis conducted. It combined 16 virtual key informant interviews, individualised written questionnaires for informants who preferred providing written responses (three in total), survey questionnaires completed by National Office representatives, document review of relevant World Vision documentation and a literature review of key academic literature on gender, VAWG, development and religion (Le Roux, 2019). The study was conducted with ethical clearance from Stellenbosch University's Research Ethics Committee: Humanities.

Chapter 8 draws on the same studies outlined in Chapter 2, primarily Pertek's PhD research projects in Turkey (Pertek, 2022a) and her experiences and learning as a practitioner at Islamic Relief Worldwide (IRW, 2015; Pertek et al., 2020) and with Islamic Relief Ethiopia (Pertek, 2020). Herein Pertek also includes the analysis from her PhD research in Tunisia (Pertek, 2022b). Overall, the chapter draws on interviews with 27 Muslim women respondents from Syria (21) and Iraq (2) living in Turkey and also four African Muslim women temporarily staying in southern Tunisia, in Medenine and Zarzis: one each from Guinea, Ivory Coast, Sierra Leone and Sudan. All respondents were survivors of multiple forms of violence and discrimination, across the continuum of forced migration, from pre-displacement, conflict, flight and into refuge. Respondents in Turkey were subjected to multiple incidents of domestic and extended family violence, while interviewees in Tunisia experienced a range of non-partner sexual violence, trafficking, kidnapping and modern slavery along their forced migration routes through the Sahel countries and Libya. Also, key informant interviews with 16 practitioners working on VAWG/ GBV in different regions, local and international organisations are included.

Using an integrated intersectional and ecological analysis, Pertek, in her studies, explored the intersection of VAWG, religion and forced displacement to identify how religion shapes displaced survivors' vulnerability and resilience to the continuum of gendered violence. In in-depth and semi-structured interviews respondents spoke about religion in response to questions concerning their resilience, coping and well-being. Local and skilled interpreters supported the interviews in Arabic and French. Throughout the research, great attention was paid to ethical considerations with regard to working with survivors of violence to ensure that engagement in research does not cause any harm and to minimise any potential emotional risks. Respondents who required material or psycho-social support were referred to local service providers. Furthermore, the safety of the researcher and interpreters was of paramount importance and was ensured by following a security protocol and limiting the number of interviews conducted each day. Ethical approval was acquired from the University of Birmingham Humanities and Social Sciences Ethical Review Committee. As in Chapter 4, the names of respondents were anonymised and pseudonyms were used. Systematic thematic analyses were deployed to process the data. Data was coded and re-coded following an inductive and iterative process until all themes were verified, merged or broken down into smaller themes, with the help of thematic maps.

The gender policy work at IRW is related to the organisation's global operations. In particular, Pertek reflected on the Gender Justice Policy of IRW (2015) and its organisational journey based on her experience as a gender and social development practitioner. The gender study, previously mentioned in Chapter 4, continues to inform Chapter 8. It was conducted in the Somali Regional State in Ethiopia, Dekasuftu Woreda, in 2015. This gender study, with details outlined in Chapter 2, included focus group discussions, key informant interviews, workshops with staff and project reports of Islamic Relief Ethiopia (Pertek, 2020).

Part III concludes with Chapter 9 ("Joint Reflection"), which uses the two preceding empirical chapters as the starting point for a more general reflection on the positive contribution of religion to VAWG prevention and response.

References

Basarudin, A. (2016). *Humanizing the sacred: Sisters in Islam and the struggle for gender justice in Malaysia.* Seattle, CA: University of Washington Press.

Beaman-Hall, L. and Nason-Clark, N. (1997). "Translating spiritual commitment into service: The response of evangelical women to wife abuse", *Canadian Woman Studies/Les Cahiers de la Femme,* 17(1): 58–62.

Beasley, M., Ochieng, D., Muyonga, I. and Kavuo, Y. (2010). "Enabling faith-based organizations to address sexual violence in schools: A case study from the democratic Republic of Congo", *Practical Theology,* 3(2): 191–202.

Bowland, S., Edmond, T. and Fallot, R.D. (2012). "Evaluation of a spiritually focused intervention with older trauma survivors", *Social Work,* 57(1): 73–82.

Bradley, T. (2010). "Religion as a bridge between theory and practice in work on violence against women in Rajasthan", *Journal of Gender Studies,* 19(4): 361–375.

Chalfant, H.P., Heller, P.L., Roberts, A., Briones, D., Aguirre-Hochbaum, S. and Farr, W. (1990). "The clergy as a resource for those encountering psychological distress", *Review of Religious Research,* 31(3): 305–313.

Drumm, R., Popescu, M., Cooper, L., Trecartin, S., Seifert, M., Foster, T. and Kilcher, C. (2014). "'God just brought me through it': Spiritual coping strategies for resilience among intimate partner violence survivors", *Clinical Social Work Journal,* 42: 385–394.

IRW. (2015). *Gender justice policy.* Birmingham: Islamic Relief Worldwide.

Le Roux, E. (2010). *An explorative baseline: The role of the church in sexual violence in countries that are/were in armed conflict, in a preventative sense and as a caring institution.* London: Tearfund.

Le Roux, E. (2014). "The role of African Christian churches in dealing with sexual violence against women: The case of the democratic Republic of Congo, Rwanda and Liberia", PhD Dissertation, Stellenbosch University.

Le Roux, E. (2018). *'Before they were in darkness, but today things have changed': Findings from a panel study with VAWG intervention participants.* London: Tearfund.

Le Roux, E. (2019). *Reflecting on the scale up project: An external study of the scale-up and adaptation of CoH G.* Seattle: World Vision International.

Le Roux, E., Corboz, J., Scott, N., Sandilands, M., Lele, U.B., Bezzolato, E. and Jewkes, R. (2020). "Engaging with faith groups to prevent VAWG in conflict-affected communities: Results from two community surveys in the DRC", *BMC International Health and Human Rights*, 20(27): 1–20.

Le Roux, E. and Palm, S. (2019). *Helping families become non-violent spaces: Exploring the roles of the Anglican Mother' Union in Zambia.* New York, NY: Episcopal Relief and Development.

Pertek, S.I. (2020). "Deconstructing Islamic perspectives on sexual and gender-based violence, toward a faith inclusive approach", in A.A. Khan and A. Cheema (eds.), *Islam and International Development: Insights for working with Muslim communities.* Rugby: Practical Action Publishing, 131–152.

Pertek, S.I. (2022a). "Religion, forced migration and the continuum of violence: An intersectional and ecological analysis", PhD Dissertation, University of Birmingham.

Pertek, S.I. (2022b). "'God helped us': Resilience, religion and experiences of gender-based violence and trafficking among African forced migrant women", *Social Sciences*, 11(5): 201.

Pertek, S.I., Almugahed, N. and Fida, N. (2020). "Integrating gender-based violence and child protection, an exploration of Islamic Relief's approaches", in K. Kraft and O.J. Wilkinson (eds.), *International development and local faith actors: Ideological and cultural encounters.* Oxon, New York, NY: Routledge, 131–152.

Raising Voices. (2016). *SASA! Faith: A training manual to prepare everyone involved in SASA! Faith.* Viewed from https://www.trocaire.org/sites/default/files/resources/policy/sasa-faith-training-manual.pdf [Date accessed: May 30, 2022].

Tomkins, A., Duff, J., Fitzgibbon, A., Karam, A., Mills, E.J., Munnings, K., Smith, S., Seshadri, S.R., Steinberg, A., Vitillo, R. and Yugi, P. (2015). "Controversies in faith and health care", *The Lancet*, 386(10005): 1776–1785.

7

A CHRISTIAN PERSPECTIVE

Drawing on religion to prevent and respond to violence against women and girls

Elisabet le Roux

Introduction

> When we decided to go through the churches, we said that if the pastor is changed and he is really involved in fighting all kind of sexual violence, he is an example of the church. It means that all the church members, those who are around the pastor, if he is engaged, it can make change, a big change in the community.
>
> *(Male NGO leader, DRC, 2010, quoted in*
> *Le Roux, 2014:116)*

This chapter explores how Christian religious actors can be agents in preventing and responding to violence against women and girls (VAWG) – as illustrated in the above quote from the DRC. Again using Ter Haar's four religious resources as framework, the chapter unpacks how the authority of the Bible as well as religious leadership can be leveraged for VAWG prevention and response, the importance of understanding and responding to religious context when working with Christian leaders and communities on addressing VAWG, and the role of prayer in VAWG prevention and

DOI: 10.4324/9781003169086-10

response. While the chapter is the result of engaging in an inductive analysis process with data from 14 different studies, this chapter uses extensive examples from only four of these studies (for more information and methodological detail on these four studies, please see Chapters 2 and 6).

Religious ideas: Drawing on the authority of the Bible

> Gender equality sends us straight to the Bible, because God created man and woman in His image and the two of them are therefore the same and are equal. If the husband deems himself higher than the woman, in that case, it is already violence. Because everyone is equal.
>
> *(Male church choir leader, DRC, 2016, quoted in Le Roux, 2018:8)*

> When (the women church leaders) were finished presenting their (Biblical) message and raising certain questions, one man, a deacon, stood up. And said, "Fine, thank you very much." And then began to challenge (the women) and to quote the scriptures on (the story of) Delilah and others to say, "You know this is how the men fell, Delilah and (the other women) seduced the men," blah blah blah blah blah. It just became such an attack, and it was so dehumanising.
>
> *(Women church leader, South Africa, interview in 2013)*

These two quotes, from two different studies on religion and VAWG (Le Roux, 2013, 2018), illustrate how the Bible contains multiple, often contradictory ideas. While the man in the first quote sees the Bible as calling for gender equality, the man described in the second quote used the Bible to justify women's inferior status. This is possible as the Bible holds "a multiplicity of traditions, which not only exist in tension with each other, but which also stand in multiple tensions with our contemporary world of life and experience" (Welker, 2003:1). One area of such tension is around gender equality and VAWG. Yet, the reality is that the Bible is an author-itative text for most Christians. If Christians believe the Bible as calling for gender equality and non-violence, the religious ideas that come from the Bible have the potential to be instrumental in countering VAWG and its consequences. Reflecting on work done with churches in Somoa, Ah Siu-Maliko et al. (2019) argue for such a scriptural approach:

> International experience suggests that biblical texts can pro-mote a significant difference within churches to attitudes and actions on VAW prevention… Work with biblical texts is critical for two reasons. First it addresses the temptation for churches to dismiss VAW prevention as a purely secular issue which is of little concern to the churches. Second, it offers generative resources to critique ways in which churches can be part of the problem, and also support discussion of ways in which churches might take leadership as part of the solution.
> *(Ah Siu-Maliko et al., 2019:7)*

A scriptural approach to VAWG prevention and response is one that relies on Biblical scriptures that underscore non-violence and women's equality, for example, Galatians 3:28 ("…there is no male and female, for you are all one in Christ Jesus"), Genesis 5:1–2 ("When God created man, he made him in the likeness of God. Male and female he created them…. and named them Man when they were created") and Proverbs 3:31 ("Do not envy the violent or choose any of their ways"). Such a scriptural approach is one that many faith-based organisations have chosen to incorporate, for in doing so their anti-VAWG messaging is supported by the authority of the Bible. An example of programming based on a scriptural approach is World Vision's Channels of Hope (CoH), a multi-day workshop focusing on a specific issue, for example, HIV and AIDS, gender, maternal and child health, or child protection. CoH is one of the key methodologies used by World Vision for mobilising reli-gious leaders and local religious communities to respond to the core issues affecting their communities. CoH Gender was developed in

2008, inspired by Elaine Pountney's book *Reclaiming the Wonder of Sexuality – A Biblical Understanding of Male and Female*. With CoH Gender, the issue of gender equality and non-violence is engaged with theologically. A process of careful and nuanced interpretation of the scriptures is facilitated to explain and promote what may be 'new' ideas concerning gender equality and non-violence to participants (Greyling, 2016). For example, the reference in Genesis 2:18 on woman being a 'helpmate' or 'helper' to the man is often used to justify women's subordinate position to men. However, an analysis of the original Hebrew term (ezer) shows that the term should rather be understood as 'lifesaver', denoting a position of coming alongside the other, and pointing to the fact that elsewhere in the Bible (Psalm 115:9–11) the same word is used to describe God. In a 2019 evaluation I conducted on the scale-up of CoH Gender, informants involved in the roll-out of CoH Gender in the various and very different settings where it had been implemented, identified the programme's engagement with the Bible as effective and appropriate. The religious content and focus of CoH Gender were appreciated by the majority of the informants, as it was seen as accurate and appropriate. They felt that the religious messaging was effective in targeting an audience that is religious and that it allows World Vision to work on a sensitive topic in a 'language' that works (Le Roux, 2019).

World Vision is not the only organisation using such a scriptural approach to VAWG prevention and response. Tearfund's 'Transforming Masculinities' approach engages with religious leaders around gender equality and non-violence through drawing on sacred texts (e.g. 1 Corinthians 12:12–27, Proverbs 31:8–10) to guide the sessions and reflections. It has been used in many parts of the world, including in the DRC, where an external evaluation affirmed the success of their intervention (Le Roux et al., 2020). Another faith-based organisation, Episcopal Relief and Development, in their work in Liberia with partner Episcopal Church of Liberia Relief and Development developed a gender-based violence toolkit *with* faith leaders that extensively engage with sacred scripture (e.g. Luke 6:36, 1 Corinthians 13:4–8) to motivate non-violence and gender equality (Le Roux and Corboz,

2019). Furthermore, in a 2017 study of five international organisations' engagement with religious leaders on harmful practices, a scriptural approach emerged as a key approach and component of four of these organisations' work with religious leaders and religious communities. Sacred scriptures usually formed the basis of an intervention, as it created a way of engaging with religious leaders in terms that they are comfortable with and trust. Used in such a way, sacred scriptures can become a powerful tool in challenging and transforming unequal and unjust structures and practices (Le Roux and Bartelink, 2017).

Scriptural engagement does not only rely on re-interpreting verses and stories of the Bible that have been used to subjugate women. It can also include intentionally focusing on pieces of scripture that actually describe (albeit often obliquely) VAWG, but have been ignored or misread. Phyllis Trible (1984) was instrumental in coining the term 'texts of terror', to refer to tales of terror with women as victims in the Bible, for example, the abused and rejected slave Hagar (Genesis 16:1–16; 21:8–21), the raped and rejected princess Tamar (2 Samuel 13), the raped and murdered concubine (Judges 19) and the killed and sacrificed virgin daughter of Jephthah (Judges 11). In her feminist engagement with these ignored scriptures, Trible used these texts of terror to "interpret stories of outrage on behalf of their female victims in order to recover a neglected history, to remember a past that the present embodies, and to pray that these terrors shall not come to pass again" (Trible, 1984:27).

A scriptural approach also offers the opportunity for interfaith collaboration in addressing VAWG. Even though different religions may rely on different sacred texts, the shared respect that they have for sacred texts may allow for interfaith collaboration. Christianity, Islam and Judaism, for example, even share certain sacred texts, and some religions emphasise the relationship and relatedness of religions that have monotheistic scriptures. This potential for interfaith collaboration was leveraged by World Vision and Islamic Relief Worldwide, when they partnered to develop a Muslim adaptation of CoH Gender. While this adaptation was not developed with the express aim of enabling interfaith CoH Gender workshops, it was an unplanned result of the process. World Vision staff in various countries indicated the need for such an interfaith version of CoH Gender in order to better serve their interfaith communities. Such 'mixed' workshops are implemented in different ways in different settings, yet all serve to promote gender equality and non-violence. With religious leaders from the two religions doing the workshop together, they develop a greater understanding of each other's religions as well as growing acknowledgement that VAWG is not just the problem of one religious group. Similarly, Tearfund has developed Muslim materials and included Qur'an scriptures and reflections to accompany the Christian content of the 'Transforming Masculinities' manual, as they were so often working in interfaith communities. With their work with HEAL Africa in the DRC, this interfaith version of Transforming Masculinities allowed their programming to work with both Christian and Muslim religious leaders. Amongst these leaders, understanding each others' religious beliefs grew to the extent that they started teaching and preaching in each others' services:

> ...last Friday at the mosque, we had an awareness campaign there, and we used a Qur'an verse that is closely related to the one in Genesis that says God created us all equal. We spoke about that last Friday. And on Sunday, our theme was gender equality. We talked about it (in the church) and we even made reference to a verse in the book of John where it says something about sexual violence, which brings havoc in many families and even in the churches.
>
> *(Male Imam, DRC, interview in 2016)*

While interfaith workshops can contribute to greater interreligious harmony and understanding, and united campaigns to address VAWG, such an interfaith approach will not always be possible to the same extent everywhere. In some countries and settings, interfaith conflict or mistrust may even prevent this option. The reality is that there is a spectrum of options lying between, on the one hand, fully integrated interfaith approaches and, on the other hand, fully separated approaches that only engage with one religious group. The appropriateness and nature of an interfaith scriptural approach will depend on the context – discussed in more detail in the next section.

In Christian communities, the religious ideas as encapsulated in the Bible therefore offers an entry point into challenging beliefs and practices that promote VAWG. To engage with sacred texts for the promotion of beliefs and principles of gender equality and non-violence is an entry point into VAWG prevention and response that is unique to religious communities.

Religious practices: The importance of understanding and responding to the context

Chapter 3's discussion of harmful religious practices might lead to the perception that all Christian practices as a whole directly or indirectly promote VAWG. But this is not the case. There are many Christian practices and rituals that promote beliefs and behaviours, such as empathy, love, kindness, and support, that are conducive to VAWG prevention and response. For example, Christian communities have a practice of tithing, which is used to support the needy; prayer is a religious practice that lies at the heart of the Christian faith and Christians are encouraged to pray for others, especially the vulnerable and destitute; and many Christian communities promote confession as a religious ritual, creating space for both perpetrators and victims of violence to speak of what they have done or experienced.

But while religious practices and rituals can therefore promote and support VAWG prevention and response, some religious practices may need some support in order to do so, as Tearfund and HEAL Africa found in the DRC. In their intervention, they trained (male and female) religious leaders on gender equality and non-violence, with the expectation that these leaders will share what they have learnt using the platforms that they have access to, for example, during sermons, group Bible Study sessions or counselling. But while Tearfund and HEAL Africa realised that church members turn to their religious leaders for counselling, they did not realise how often this happens. It was the research accompanying the intervention that revealed how often people, and especially couples, go to religious leaders for counselling. The baseline qualitative research showed that all of the religious leaders that formed part of the panel study had counselled one or more couples in the preceding six months, and that, overall, the vast majority of the counselling that they do is with couples. Furthermore, even people who do not belong to the religious leader's church, or even to any faith group, will approach religious leaders for counselling.

However, the research accompanying the intervention revealed that this counselling at times has quite a moralistic tone, with the religious leaders imparting advice, rather than listening and facilitating dialogue between partners. For example, in 2017 a male lay leader within a Pentecostal church described as follows the counselling he gave a couple who was fighting because of the husband's alcohol abuse: "I tried to quote them all the violence: economic violence, physical violence and several other forms of violence. I have quoted them the ways of managing assets in the home. Threats are not good; I told them like that" (quoted in Le Roux, 2018:24). Furthermore, reflecting on the counselling advice the religious leaders reported giving to couples, it was clear that the continuation of the marriage was of utmost importance for the religious leaders. Irrespective of the problems a couple was having, the counselling process would push for reconciliation. This is why HEAL Africa and Tearfund arranged a special training on counselling for selected religious leaders. These trainings were not only aimed at strengthening these leaders' counselling skills (through active listening, empathy, nonverbal communication, etc.), but again worked with religious leaders on how their religion promotes gender equality and non-violence and how this applies to counselling couples.

This example illustrates how religious practices can promote VAWG prevention and responses, but may at times require support in order to do so effectively. The support that is needed will depend on the context, for religious practices differ in their nature and meaning, depending on context. Even within the same religion, or even the same denomination, religious practices are not always the same, are not enacted in the same ways and do not always have the same meaning. The research I did for World Vision on their scaled-up use of CoH Gender serves as a good illustration of the importance of taking context into account.

In October 2013, World Vision started a five-year, externally funded project entitled 'Channels of Hope Gender Scale Up Project'. A total of 18 countries were involved in the Scale Up Project: Armenia, Bolivia, Burundi, El Salvador, Ethiopia, Kenya, Lesotho, Malawi, Peru, Pacific Timor-Leste (Papua New Guinea, Solomon Islands), South Sudan, South Africa, Tanzania, Uganda, Zambia, Zimbabwe, Guatemala and Nicaragua. In the 2019 external evaluation I conducted of this CoH Gender implementation in 18 very different settings, the critical importance of understanding, respecting and adapting to the local religious context emerged strongly. A church in Peru is not the same as a church in South Africa. Even within the same denominations there are often marked differences. Of course, it is not only religious practices that may differ but also religious ideas, organisation and experiences. As was illustrated through the implementation of CoH Gender in the 18 countries, it is critically important to fully understand the local religious context and design VAWG prevention and response programming that responds to this understanding and is therefore appropriate. For example, where there were local religious sensitivities to the word 'gender' the methodology was renamed (e.g. 'Relationships in Harmony' and 'CoH Family'); in other settings the language and theological concepts and content of CoH Gender were simplified. In Armenia, a fairly comprehensive adaptation of CoH Gender was needed in order to make it responsive to and usable in the Armenian Orthodox Church context. By 2019, WVI had commissioned four independent studies of CoH Gender (Wilson and Bartelink, 2014; Wu and Kilby, 2015; Le Roux and Olivier, 2017; Meyer and Nikulainen, 2018) and all four studies emphasised the importance of contextualising CoH Gender to the setting where it will be implemented in order to ensure uptake of gender equality and non-violent messaging.

Especially when working on VAWG, with the sensitivities there are around gender, sex, relationships and violence, the need to engage sensitively and appropriately is crucial. In order to design and implement VAWG interventions that effectively work with religious leaders and communities, religious literacy has to be more than merely understanding the basic tenets and practices of the religion/s that are engaged with. Rather,

> ...it includes an understanding of the role of religion and religious actors in a given community. Thus it looks at religion within the context of a particular community, at a given time, and considers culture (including cultural norms and practices around gender), ethnicity, history, etc. And it is not a knowledge that one can obtain in a course and then be "religiously literate;" it is a skillset, or toolbox, that enables people... to gain the relevant knowledge and understanding in the places that they work.
>
> *(Gingerich et al., 2017:18)*

Understanding and responding to context is clearly not only relevant to leveraging religious practices for VAWG prevention and response. A thorough understanding of the religious landscape that you are entering is crucial to being able to engage with it successfully around VAWG prevention and response.

Religious organisation: Leveraging religious leadership

Christian churches, irrespective of denomination, almost always have a strongly hierarchical organisational structure. The Roman Catholic Church is arguably the most well-known example of the hierarchical nature of churches: the pope is the head of the Catholic Church globally; the thousands of Catholic dioceses worldwide are each headed by a bishop; and each diocese is divided into a number of parishes, each headed by a priest (or a deacon or lay minister, if a priest is not available). But it is not only mainstream churches with a global presence that have such hierarchical organisational structures, for even small, independent churches usually have a strict hierarchy. Clergy generally have much power and influence, seeing that the organisational structure of the church tends to assign them such power and influence. This was, for example, illustrated in an anonymous survey completed as part of a study on African Christian leadership. Eight thousand forty-one adult Christians (the majority of whom were Protestant) across Kenya, Angola and the Central African Republic (CAR) were asked to name the Christian person outside of their family who has been most influential on them. 75.7% of the CAR respondents, 69.9% of the Kenyan respondents and 58.6% of the Angolan respondents indicated that it was a pastor or other church leader (Gitau, 2017).

Considering their power within churches' organisational structure, and the influence that they have on church members and often the wider community as well, religious leaders have significant potential in addressing VAWG. Immersed and part of the communities that they serve, religious leaders are respected and trusted by their religious community, understand the developmental challenges and concerns within their community and have significant reach and influence because of the size of their constituencies (Thomson, 2014). Religious leaders act as gatekeepers into a community, allowing discussion and response to VAWG; they can leverage their influence, trust networks and infrastructure to address VAWG; and they can draw on a range of religious resources and authority (e.g. prayers, sermons, sacred texts and rituals) that can be used to address the drivers and consequences of VAWG (Palm and Eyber, 2019). Again, I turn to Tearfund and HEAL Africa's work in the DRC to illustrate how the reach and influence of religious leaders can support VAWG prevention and response.

The project focused on addressing VAWG, and especially sexual violence, through engaging with religious communities and their leaders (both Muslim and Christian, and engaging various Christian denominations, including catholic, protestant, evangelical and pentecostal). The qualitative research accompanying the intervention captured how the religious leaders experienced being part of the intervention, highlighting that the intervention was able to bring personal change in their attitudes and behaviours, leverage their existing influence and platforms and motivate them to mobilise within their communities:

We have found that this awareness has changed us within our own households as couples and from there we went to the community....From what I am seeing, as I said, it started transforming my household because we are a couple. The wife also participates in the awareness at church. I have realised that I have also changed. When she changed, I changed and so did the children.

(Male lay church leader, DRC, 2016, quoted in Le Roux, 2018:14)

Before I (conduct a session), I need to prepare myself and put myself on this subject. For example, as I'm talking about social norms, are there changes in my own house? So that I can now go and teach the others? It is better that changes exist first in my house. I need to be a (role)model.

(Female lay church leader, DRC, 2017, quoted in Le Roux, 2018:14)

The aim of the project was not only to transform and equip religious leaders but also that they in turn transform their communities. The key starting assumption of the project was that religious leaders can drive change around VAWG at community level. In the qualitative research accompanying the project, community members reported being part of discussions (hosted by religious leaders) on gender equality and non-violence, and how it impacted them. For example, some disclosed:

I was abusive on economic violence aspect; even physical violence. After that teaching I live in peace with my wife at home.

(Male church member, DRC, interview in 2016)

When I heard the teaching, first of all I felt that it is a good teaching as for my family it helps to make sure we help each other... What touched me is that when you are a father in a family you must not let anger control you; and don't have a habit of beating people physically. Also, you should not react in a way that can harm somebody physically. Well, I saw that it can be a good thing helping people to live in peace in marriage.

(Male church member, DRC, interview in 2016)

These male church members' experiences were affirmed by the endline evaluation, which showed significantly more equitable gender attitudes and less tolerance for interpersonal violence at endline, a positive shift across the entire community in terms of gender attitudes, rape myths and rape stigma scores, and a significant decline in all aspects of intimate-partner violence. These results indicate the capacity and influence of religious leaders and religious communities in general, suggesting that "working with faith leaders and faith communities as an entry point into communities is a strategic approach and can impact the entire community" (Le Roux et al., 2020:18).

It is important to note that this intervention, while prioritising religious leaders, did not only engage with formal clergy. On the contrary, it intentionally also worked with those women and men in informal leadership positions within their respective churches, for example, choir leaders, catechists, intercessors, youth leaders and readers. If the intervention worked only with the top-level religious leaders within churches, it would have meant that it would engage almost only with older, male Christian leaders. But by including lay leaders from churches, they could include youth and women. While these lay leaders are filling voluntary, informal roles, all of them are recognised as leaders within their churches.

It was important to intentionally include these lay leaders, for otherwise the intervention could easily reinforce patriarchal power structures, as formal religious leadership is usually only male. A 2016 study by the Pew Research Centre on the gender gap in religion around the world found that, while women are generally more religious than men, this is especially true with Christian women. Among Christians, women are more religious than men on all measures of religious practice, commitment and belief (Pew Research Center, 2016). Furthermore, while church membership differs based on denomination and country, there is consensus that church membership globally is predominantly female. Yet women are rarely the leaders of churches (Adams, 2007; Hendriks, 2012; Madimbo, 2012; Ngunjiri and Christo-Baker, 2012; Ngunjiri et al., 2012). Women leaders in church are said to be facing the 'stained-glass ceiling', which prohibits their rise within leadership structures (De Four-Babb and Tenia, 2012; Kwaka-Sumba and Le Roux, 2017; Sullins, 2000); others explain that women religious leaders have to navigate a labyrinth, a metaphor for the complex journey that requires persistence, focus and creativity in order to overcome the religious and traditional doctrines and practices that limit them (Eagly and Carli, 2007; Klenke, 2011). While compared to churches like the Roman Catholic Church, churches such as African Independent Churches and Pentecostal Churches tend to create more room for women leaders (Mapuranga, 2013), the majority of church leaders – and especially formal, paid church leaders – remain men (see e.g. Hendriks, 2012). This is a major concern in terms of including religious leaders in VAWG prevention and response work, for engaging religious leadership may then inadvertently strengthen the power and privilege of men. Within the VAWG prevention movement there is a strong resistance to what is perceived by many as a male co-opting of the violence prevention space, with legitimate concerns about how it may simply repackage and promote patriarchal ideas on what is needed to end VAWG (Walsh, 2015; COFEM, 2017).

Therefore, it is important to look further than only the top-level, formal religious leaders within churches. One way, as illustrated in the DRC, is to also engage with informal, lay leadership. Another way to avoid reinforcing patriarchal power hierarchies is to intentionally seek out women's spaces within churches and to find the leaders within these spaces. An example of such a space within the Anglican Church is the Mothers' Union. Research conducted in 2018–2019 with the Mothers' Union in Zambia (MUZ) revealed how influential the leaders of this women's organisation are. The MUZ members and leaders that took part in focus groups and interviews emphasised that one of the organisation's key functions is to create a space where members receive teaching on a wide range of issues (e.g. child rearing, conflict management, the Bible and cooking). They are thus expecting their leaders to increase their knowledge and also guide their beliefs and behaviours. While the research did complexify the nature of the teaching being provided within the MUZ – which is not always conducive to gender equality and non-violence – it is undeniable that this is a space where religious women are taught, influenced and led by *women religious leaders*. In the Zambian Anglican Church, the Mothers' Union and its leaders also have considerable influence within the wider church, partly since it is such an old church ministry and also because there are more women within the church and they are generally more active members than the men. Thus, while the MUZ chapter in each church does not function independently of the priest at the helm of the church, it nevertheless has considerable influence. The Mothers' Union is not the only such religious women's space. For example, within the Anglican Church in Zambia, there are two other women's organisations, namely St Veronica's and Young Families.

Another way to ensure that programming does not inadvertently reinforce existing patriarchal power hierarchies is to identify those church leaders who are already working on gender and VAWG-related issues. For example, in research conducted with religious leaders in Colombia within six internally displaced communities, it was the women church leaders who showed the most awareness of sexual violence and had the most drive for responding to it, and these were usually informal church leaders who ran the children's or women's ministries. Looking for religious leaders passionate about addressing VAWG, and those already working to address it, will usually mean finding female religious leaders (Le Roux and Cadavid Valencia, 2020).

As this section discussed, religious leaders can be key partners in VAWG prevention and response because of their reach and influence within the church as a whole, but often also the wider community. At the same time, such engagement should avoid blindly reinforcing existing patriarchal power hierarchies by (simplistically) only engaging with the top-level leaders within churches. As these are usually men, effort must be put into identifying the lay leaders and alternative spaces where informal women religious leaders operate, and women and their issues are prioritised and addressed.

Religious experience: The transformative power of prayer

Prayer is an important religious practice within the Christian tradition. However, prayer itself can also be or lead to religious experiences that are transformative and empowering. In this section I discuss how prayer's transformative power can contribute to VAWG prevention and response.

In 2010 I conducted explorative research on the role of churches in addressing sexual violence against women in communities affected by armed conflict, doing fieldwork in two communities each in three countries (the DRC, Rwanda and Liberia). Amongst other things, one nominal group session was conducted in each community. The Nominal Group Technique is a consensus method aimed at problem-solving, idea-generation or determining priorities. Group members are asked a question and then, in a four-stage process, asked to individually generate ideas, share the ideas, clarify the ideas and then as a group rank the ideas (McMillan et al., 2016). Group members in the DRC, Rwanda and Liberia were men and women of different ages and from different churches (including catholic, protestant, evangelical and pentecostal churches), as nominal group sessions can ensure balanced participation from all group members. In the nominal group sessions I conducted, the group members were asked to answer the question "What should the church be doing about sexual violence?" Group members were encouraged to think practically and creatively to come up with, and then select, the activities that they think are the most important for churches to engage in.

In both communities in both Liberia and Rwanda, the groups voted that the most important thing for churches to do about sexual violence was to pray; in one of the communities in the DRC, prayer was the fourth-most voted for activity. While all of the groups came up with many other practical suggestions (e.g. providing food and accommodation for survivors), the majority of the nominal groups nevertheless indicated that prayer remains the most important thing that churches should be doing about sexual violence. In the interviews and group sessions with church leaders and members, the need for prayer was reiterated. For example, a session with a group of church leaders in the DRC came up with a list of practical activities that churches should be doing about sexual violence. Yet the leaders kept emphasising the need for prayer. As one of these religious leaders explained (DRC, interview in 2010): "We need to pray, because it is God alone who can end this problem… We can come out of this situation through prayer only". The transformative power of prayer was seen as fundamentally important to bringing the needed change. This was not a fatalistic approach, where prayer is turned to because nothing else is working, for in all three countries the respondents also expected churches to do other practical things, too. Rather, prayer appears to have been emphasised as it has a particular power and influence, without which fundamental change (of individuals and the community) will be impossible.

For survivors, prayer can also be a transformational religious experience, helping them deal with the consequences of the violence they experienced. For example, survivors pray to God to help them forget bad memories and help them focus on their future and not what has happened to them (Smigelsky et al., 2017). They experience prayer, through God, as bringing this change in their thinking and emotional struggles. Through prayer, a survivor can also experience connection with God, which supports and heals them in a way that human interaction often does not (Knapik et al., 2008). Prayer can therefore be a transformative, healing experience for survivors.

Yet prayer is often-times understood as a delegation of responsibility to a divine figure or as a simplistic coping mechanism through which those who are suffering feel less vulnerable (Probasco, 2016). Such understandings of prayer can lead to it being dismissed as a trick or mechanism to help the pray-er deal with challenging circumstances. The power of prayer is often ignored, as is the fact that, for many, it has been and can be a transformative experience. For example, in her study of how prayer is understood within

International Relations as a discipline, Schwarz argues that scholars (not limited to International Relations) rely on ontologies of religious practices that lead them to:

> ...treat prayer as an emotional and irrational practice that is engaged with the human mind (as opposed to the body), focused on private matters of religious faith (as opposed to reason), only concerned with the transcendental (instead of the immanent), and analytically and materially separated from real action or work.
>
> *(Schwarz, 2018:35)*

Ellis and Ter Haar (2004, 2007), in their study of religion in Africa, argue that religion and religious practices such as prayer can be political acts of empowerment. This is, they argue, as Africans see the invisible world as being the origin of all power and spiritual power as real and effective power (Ellis and Ter Haar, 2007). Prayer is therefore a real and practical action through which the pray-er enacts and leverages power. Other scholars have also drawn attention to prayer being an act of agency, premised on the pray-er's belief in their power to influence a divine being (Probasco, 2016).

By ignoring the potential of prayer as a religious experience, we ignore the role that it can play in VAWG prevention and response. It is important to "take a reflexive approach to religion, avoiding the essentialisation of 'religious' phenomena and instead closely examining the meanings and roles they take on for the subjects themselves, as well as how such practices inform specific strategies, identities, and projects" (Schwarz, 2018:50).

Conclusion

As this chapter has illustrated, different religious resources connected to Christianity can form part of VAWG prevention and response in different ways. When VAWG prevention and response messaging draws on the authority of the Bible, there is added motivation for Christian leaders and Christian communities to take new ideas seriously, and it is an effective and unique entry point when addressing VAWG. Reflecting on religious practices highlights that understanding and responding to context is critically important when working with Christian communities. Within Christian churches in the African contexts examined, there is almost always a strongly hierarchical leadership structure and the leaders of the church have much influence and authority. This influence and authority can be leveraged for VAWG prevention and response if leaders can be convinced of the importance of doing such work, and the risk of inadvertently support existing patriarchal power structures is avoided. Finally, for many Christians, including survivors, there is a very real understanding that prayer can bring profound change in a community and in an individual. This experience of prayer can become part of VAWG prevention and response. Therefore, while Chapter 3 discussed key ways in which Christian beliefs, practices, organisational structures and experiences can lead to VAWG and counter prevention and response efforts, it is not the whole story. As this chapter has illustrated, there are many dimensions to Christianity and Christian communities that can be conducive to and influential in VAWG prevention and response.

References

Adams, J. (2007). "Stained glass makes the ceiling visible: Organisational opposition to women in congregational leadership", *Gender and Society*, 21(1): 80–105.

Ah Siu-Maliko, M., Beres, M., Blyth, C., Boodoosingh, R., Patterson, T. and Tombs, D. (2019). *Church responses to gender-based violence against women in Samoa*. New Zealand Institute for Pacific Research. Viewed from http://hdl.handle.net/10523/9657 [Date accessed: April 6, 2022].

COFEM. (2017). *Reframing the language of 'gender-based violence' away from feminist underpinnings*. Feminist Perspectives on Addressing Violence against Women and Girls Series, Paper No. 2. Viewed from https://cofemsocialchange.org/wp-content/uploads/2018/11/Paper-2-Reframing-language-of-%E2%80%98GBV%E2%80%99-away-from-feminist-underpinnings.pdf [Date accessed: April 6, 2022].

De Four-Babb, J. and Tenia, S.-A. (2012). "From the pantry to the pulpit: Anglican clergywomen in the Diocese of Trinidad and Tobago", *The Journal of Pan African Studies*, 5(2): 42–66.

Eagly, A.H. and Carli, L.L. (2007). *Through the labyrinth: The truth about how women become leaders*. Boston, MA: Harvard Business Press.

Ellis, S. and Ter Haar, G. (2004). *Worlds of power: Religious thought and political practice in Africa.* Johannesburg: Wits University Press.

Ellis, S. and Ter Haar, G. (2007). "Religion and politics: Taking African epistemologies seriously", *Journal of Modern African Studies*, 45(3): 385–401.

Gingerich, T.R., Moore, D.L., Brodrick, R. and Beriont, C. (2017). *Local humanitarian leadership and religious literacy: Engaging with religion, faith, and faith actors.* Harvard Divinity School Religious Literacy Project. Viewed from https://www.oxfam.org/en/research/local-humanitarian-leadership-and-religious-literacy [Date accessed: September 7, 2022].

Gitau, W.M. (2017). "Formation of African Christian leaders: Patterns from the ALS Data", in R.J. Priest and K. Barine (eds.), *African Christian leadership: Realities, opportunities, and impact.* New York, NY: Orbis Books, 49–64.

Greyling, C. (2016). "Crossing faith boundaries: Channels of hope and world vision", in A. Ware and M. Clarke (eds.), *Development across faith boundaries.* Abingdon: Routledge, 67–82.

Hendriks, H.J. (2012). "Churches, seminaries and gender statistics", in H.J. Hendriks, E. Mouton, L. Hansen and E. Le Roux (eds.), *Men in the pulpit, women in the pew? Addressing gender inequality in Africa.* Stellenbosch: SunPress, 25–32.

Klenke, K. (2011). *Women in leadership: Contextual dynamics and boundaries.* Bingley: Emerald Group Publishing Limited.

Knapik, G.P., Martsolf, D.S. and Draucker, C.B. (2008). "Being delivered: Spirituality in survivors of sexual violence", *Issues in Mental Health Nursing*, 29(4): 335–350.

Kwaka-Sumba, T. and Le Roux, E. (2017). "African women leadership: Realities and opportunities", in R.J. Priest and K. Barine (eds.), *African Christian leadership: Realities, opportunities, and impact.* New York, NY: Orbis Books, 135–153.

Le Roux, E. (2013). *Sexual violence in South Africa and the role of the Church.* Viewed from http://learn.tearfund.org/~/media/Files/TILZ/HIV/Breaking_the_silenceweb_FINAL.pdf?la=en [Date accessed: March 15, 2018].

Le Roux, E. (2014). "The role of African Christian churches in dealing with sexual violence against women: The case of the democratic Republic of Congo, Rwanda and Liberia", PhD Dissertation, Stellenbosch University.

Le Roux, E. (2018). *'Before they were in darkness, but today things have changed': Findings from a panel study with VAWG intervention participants.* London: Tearfund.

Le Roux, E. (2019). *Reflecting on the scale up project: An external study of the scale-up and adaptation of CoH G*. Seatttle: World Vision International.

Le Roux, E. and Bartelink, B.E. (2017). *No more 'harmful traditional practices': Working effectively with faith leaders*. Joint Learning Initiative on Faith and Local Communities. Viewed from https://jliflc.com/resources/ no-harmful-traditional-practices-working-effectively-faith-leaders/ [Date accessed: September 7, 2022]

Le Roux, E. and Cadavid Valencia, L. (2020). "Partnering with local faith communities: Learning from the response to internal displacement and sexual violence in Colombia", in K. Kraft and O.J. Wilkinson (eds.), *International development and local faith actors: Ideological and cultural encounters*. Oxon: Routledge, 236–250.

Le Roux, E. and Corboz, J. (2019). *Baseline report: Engaging faith-based organizations to prevent violence against women and girls*. New York: Episcopal Relief & Development.

Le Roux, E., Corboz, J., Scott, N., Sandilands, M., Lele, U.B., Bezzolato, E. and Jewkes, R. (2020). "Engaging with faith groups to prevent VAWG in conflict-affected communities: Results from two community surveys in the DRC", *BMC International Health and Human Rights*, 20(27): 1–20.

Le Roux, E. and Olivier, J. (2017). *Channels of hope in practice: A study of channels of hope gender implementation in two countries*. Johannesburg: World Vision.

Madimbo, M. (2012). "Supportive leadership behaviour key to breaking the glass ceiling in religious communities in Malawi", *Journal of Pan African Studies*, 5(2): 27–41.

Mapuranga, T.P. (2013). "Bargaining with patriarchy? Women pentecostal leaders in Zimbabwe", *Fieldwork in Religion*, 8(1): 74–91.

McMillan, S.S., King, K. and Tully, M.P. (2016). "How to use the nominal group and Delphi techniques", *International Journal of Clinical Pharmacy*, 38: 655–662.

Meyer, A. and Nikulainen, E. (2017). *Evaluation report: PTL reducing gender based violence project*. World Vision and FinnOC.

Ngunjiri, F.W. and Christo-Baker, E.A. (2012). "Breaking the stained glass ceiling: African women's leadership in religious organizations", *The Journal of Pan African Studies*, 5(2): 1–4.

Ngunjiri, F.W., Gramby-Sobukwe, S. and Williams-Gegner, K. (2012). "Tempered radicals: Black women's leadership in the church and community", *Journal of Pan African Studies*, 5(2): 84–109.

Palm, S. and Eyber, C. (2019). *Why faith? Engaging the mechanisms of faith to end violence against children*. Joint Learning Initiative on Faith and Local Communities. Viewed from https://jliflc.com/resources/

why-faith-engaging-faith-mechanisms-to-end-violence-against-children/ [Date accessed: April 6, 2022].

Pew Research Center. (2016). *The gender gap in religion around the world.* Pew Research Center. Viewed from https://www.pewforum. org/2016/03/22/the-gender-gap-in-religion-around-the-world/ [Date accessed: March 1, 2022].

Pountney, E.R. (2008). *Reclaiming the wonder of sexuality: Toward a biblical understanding of male and female.* Bloomington, IN: Trafford.

Probasco, L. (2016). "Prayer, patronage, and personal agency in Nicaraguan accounts of receiving international aid", *Journal for the Scientific Study of Religion*, 55(2): 233–249.

Schwarz, T.B. (2018). "Challenging the ontological boundaries of religious practices in international relations scholarship", *International Studies Review*, 20: 30–54.

Smigelsky, M.A., Gill, A.R., Foshager, D., Aten, J.D. and Im, H. (2017). "'My heart is in his hands': The lived spiritual experiences of Congolese refugee women survivors of sexual violence", *Journal of Prevention and Intervention in the Community*, 45(4): 261–273.

Sullins, P. (2000). "The stained glass ceiling: Career attainment for women clergy", *Sociology of Religion*, 61(3): 243–266.

Thomson, J. (2014). "Local faith actors and protection in complex and insecure environments", *Forced Migration Review*, 48: 5–6.

Trible, P. (1984). *Texts of terror: Literary-feminist readings of biblical narratives.* Philadelphia, PA: Fortress.

Walsh, S. (2015). "Addressing sexual violence and rape culture: Issues and interventions targeting boys and men", *Agenda*, 29(3): 134–141.

Welker, M. (2003). "Sola scriptura? The authority of the Bible in pluralistic environments", in B.A. Strawn, P.D. Miller and N.R. Bowen (eds.), *A god so near: Essays on old testament theology in honor of Patrick D. Miller.* Winona Lake, IN: Eisenbrauns, 375–391.

Wilson, E.K. and Bartelink, B.E. (2014). *Evaluation report of channels of hope for gender.* World Vision.

Wu, J. and Kilby, P. (2015). *Evaluation of Honiara community vision for change project.* World Vision Solomon Islands.

8

A MUSLIM PERSPECTIVE

Religion as protective resource in violence against women and girls

Sandra Iman Pertek

Introduction

> Islam didn't permit men to abuse us, but it's because they are unfair people. Allah said to us that we should be patient and encourage others to be patient, and Allah is so merciful.
>
> (Emina from Syria, quoted in Pertek, 2022a:342)

The above statement was shared with me during my fieldwork in Ankara (Turkey), where survivors argued that violence was not part of their religion, and such a belief empowered them to resist violence. Refugee women, I interviewed, insisted that these were rather people who have distorted the true religious beliefs and ideals, which has led to violence against women and girls (VAWG). In this chapter, I explore ways in which religious resources can operate as protective factors in VAWG and support survivors. The discussion is again structured around Ter Haar's religious resources, centring on those resources that protect women's and girls' dignity. Drawing on data collected in Turkey and Tunisia (Pertek, 2022a), I begin by highlighting the vital functions of religious beliefs in meaning-making and resistance building; religious practices in

DOI: 10.4324/9781003169086-11

enabling survivors to cope with violence; and religious experiences in empowering and healing of survivors. I explore how religious organisations and communities deploy their different religious resources to counter VAWG by drawing on my practical experience from a gender policy advisory role and programming in international development.

Religious ideas: Meaning-making and resistance building

Religious beliefs can help women survivors make sense of their experiences and build resistance to gendered violence. Levantine refugee women I met in Turkey relied on their religious thinking frameworks, and faith-inspired narratives of justice, to deal with the VAWG they were experiencing or had experienced. With their support networks destroyed or ruptured due to displacement, they described their religious beliefs and traditions as their only 'weapon' against abusive husbands and non-partner perpetrators. Religious beliefs helped these women to resist violence and challenge patriarchal religious interpretations that enabled discrimination and abuse.

Women deployed their beliefs in three powerful ways. First, there were those who used religious sources – *hadiths* and Qur'an – to argue against women's submissiveness and secondary position in society. Syrian women, for example, reinterpreted the contentious Qur'anic verses (e.g. 4:34 discussed in Chapter 4), contesting male interpretations which may imply women's subordination. They resisted submissiveness and challenged abuse by reverting to their own reading of the Qur'an and the Prophetic tradition, wherein they found a sacred value of women and interpretations condemning violence against them. Such processes of critical reinterpretation empowered survivors to imagine for themselves and their spouses a non-violent future in honourable relationships in line with their beliefs. As one respondent shared:

> The prophet said: "Take my advice with regard to women: Act kindly"...If the woman did something wrong, then religion says: "[a woman] must be retained in honour or released

in kindness". This is what should happen if we can no longer tolerate each other…

> (*Zainab from Syria, quoted in Pertek, 2022a:226–227*)

Second, there were some women who understood and explained men as misusing religious sources. Survivors who felt literate in their faith (by knowing religious teachings, ethics and the religious scriptures) questioned men's ability in the wider community to correctly interpret sacred texts. Some women described men from their religious and ethnic communities as reading sacred texts literally, without the knowledge, and being unwilling to engage in the needed processes of interpretation. A number of survivors challenged, specifically, the contentious Qur'anic verse 4:34, which was used by men out of context to reinforce patriarchal social norms:

> This Surah [Chapter], they didn't complete the Surah until the end, they just took these three words '*Alrrijalu qawwa-moona Aala alnnisai'* [men are the protectors/maintainers of women] and make their religion rule to control women. Also, the Prophet PBUH said, 'the best of you is the best for their family' and that means his wife, and he said in his last sermon, 'you should do the best for your women'.
>
> (*Sara from Syria, quoted in Pertek, 2022a:227*)

Some survivors described their spouses as non-practising, irreligious men who in the process of misunderstanding scriptures were enabled to perpetrate harm. These women interpreted that the violence being experienced actually has nothing to do with religion, but is due to not practising religion. Respondents often recalled the religious concept of '*haram*' – prohibited acts – when referring to a woman's mistreatment and argued to protect women's rights enshrined in Islam. They believed that a return to 'pure religion', that is, the fundamental Qur'anic principles and the Prophetic guidance, would lead to an end in VAWG.

> That [VAWG] is because our community is very behind the times and very tough one…I think the cure is to go back to the true *Sunnah* and the true meaning behind the *Surah*

[chapter] in Qur'an…But at this time, with songs, nightclubs, television, and the internet it is very hard.

(Fardous from Syria, interview in 2019)

Most women subjected to domestic abuse argued that Islam protected them from violence, condemned violence and promoted gender equality. This finding is supported by Ghafournia's (2017) study with Muslim immigrant women in Australia who believed that their experiences of abuse and violence stem from breaching religious concepts and not practising one's religion. One respondent in her Australian study said: "I just know that I feel what people are doing in the name of Islam is different from what God or his Prophet really want and say… Now they use whatever is beneficial for them" (Zeinab from Iraq in Ghafournia, 2017:155). Although most interviewed women in Ghafournia's study (2017) differentiated between the Islamic values and cultural beliefs that delayed their response to abuse, some women equated culture with religion and blamed both as barriers to help-seeking. Such findings highlight that VAWG interventions should deploy accurate analysis of the religion–culture and gender nexus with other socio-economic drivers of violence to address VAWG's root causes effectively.

Third, drawing upon the Prophetic traditions (*hadiths* – narrations of Prophetic sayings), religious refugee survivors in Turkey contested patriarchal interpretations of 'abused verses' and did not equate men's responsibility for women's protection and maintenance with control. Several survivors, drawing upon their religious knowledge, reminded their abusive husbands about the Prophetic advice of how to treat women:

> …when he beats me, I ask, "does your religion permit you to do this?" and he says yes and that God made it obligatory for women to obey their husbands, but they forget that God ordered husbands to be good men and treat their women fairly…I told him that the Prophet never hit his wives, but he told me I am not the Prophet…
>
> *(Maya from Syria, quoted in Pertek, 2022a:150)*

Many Muslim communities believe in the liberatory properties of the Qur'an which aimed to end the oppression and injustice against women in the 7th-century Arabia, where Muslims believe the Qur'an was revealed. While the widespread misogynist and historical Islamic interpretations cannot be denied, contemporarily the Qur'an is perceived by many Muslim women through feminist and rights-based perspective (e.g. Musawah Movement), emphasising their legal, socio-economic and family rights as important provisions granted to them 13 centuries before feminist movements. Islamic feminists and contemporary Muslim scholars believe that strong emancipatory feminist strains present within Islamic scholarship can revive the concept of gender equality in Islam, based on a faith-inspired framework of gender justice (see Mernissi, 1991; Ahmed, 1992; Ashrof, 2005; Mir-Hosseini, 2006; Wadud, 2006). Their efforts contest patriarchal influences and traditionalist interpretations that may produce and legitimise violence against women with the independent analysis of religious sources (*ijtihad*) and interpretation of the Qur'an (*tafsir*) (Minganti, 2015).

Religious practices: Praying and reading scriptures to cope

Among the women I met in Turkey and Tunisia, reliance on religious practices – individual prayers and reading religious scripts – were frequently discussed as an important part of survivors' coping strategies (Pertek, 2022a, 2022b). Refugee religious women relied especially on prayers and the recalling of religious texts to build their mental resistance against violence. Several studies have demonstrated how religious women resist gendered violence in their lives with the help of their religious beliefs (Hassouneh-Phillips, 2003; Ghafournia, 2017). For instance, in the study of Zakar et al. (2012), survivors of domestic violence in Pakistan used prayers and communal religious places to seek protection from violence. In one respondent's account her abusive husband suspended abuse during her prayers due to the respect for this religious practice (ibid.).

Prayers enhanced victims' coping capacities and buffered against psychological distress, helping them relieve anxiety and stress (Rutledge et al., 2021). Survivors prayed for protection, to exit from abusive relationships, and for life change because they believed only prayers can change their situations. Obligatory and voluntary prayers, at different times of the day and night, provided women with comfort, stabilised their emotions and relieved anxieties. Prayers also helped women to manage their stress by distracting themselves from their daily worries about their past and future. Sending blessings on the Prophet multiple times and keeping an ablution (*wudo* − ritual purification) helped Muslim respondents to feel at peace. A prayer, especially when bowing (*sujūd*), helped women to gain clarity in their thoughts, comfort and find solutions to their problems. Also, in sadness and anxiety Muslim women reported reliance on bead prayers (*dhikr*) to help alleviate their painful recurring memories, for example, of trafficking or deceased family members. They followed a daily routine of supplications and Qur'an recitation, the daily morning and evening devotions to occupy and pass time with positive spiritual effects, which helped to manage their anxiety, as source of peace:

> When I am in *Sujūd* [bowing] I feel a connection to Allah… Every morning when I wake up, I say: *"La Hawla Wala Quwwata Illa Billah"* [there is no might nor power except with Allah]…400 times, and seeking forgiveness 100 times, and sending blessings upon the Prophet 100 times, and I like reading *Ayat Al-Kursi*; when I read it, it brings me peace and relief. It became like a daily habit, I'd recite all of these with the prayer beads, and then I'd feel comfortable afterwards…
>
> *(Lotifa from Syria, quoted in Pertek, 2022a:231)*

According to service providers that were interviewed, the ritual daily prayers (that occur five times every day) were for many forced migrant survivors their only lifeline in their extreme hardships. A service provider in Iraq explained that women may delay disclosure and help-seeking for years, but that this did not mean they did not disclose to anyone. They disclosed the abuse to God, seeking justice, protection and prayed against their perpetrators. Connecting with God, through prayers, helped survivors put their life into perspective with hope:

> The religion is like a rope for them to hold on and it gives them peace, it gives them hope, it keeps them be alive, and it keeps them going...their faith and belief plays a very important role in holding themselves together...Most of the cases are reported after maybe one year...or maybe three to five years...in this period, they are managing these things on their own...and this is the point when they are having faith and are believing in God – 'that person will be punished by God...'
>
> *(Zara, GBV Coordinator in Iraq, FBO-INGO,*
> *interview in 2019)*

Moreover, the Levantine respondents relied on the memorised verses or reading certain chapters of the Qur'an daily, finding therein comfort, confidence and peace. Many sought guidance and hope in the religious text when coping with abuse and when working to rebuild their lives. Some sought protection within the Qur'an, for example, by playing its audio recordings while they slept or by reciting the Qur'anic chapters for their protection properties (e.g. Chapter *'Al-Kahf'* and 'The Cave'). For many Muslims, the melodic nature of Qur'anic recitation inspires comfort and was used by survivors of violence for healing (Hassouneh-Phillips, 2003). Respondents who engaged with a religious text believed they talked to God directly, as if they were reading/hearing God's own words. Some even rejected institutionalised mediators:

> Because my book is here, my religion is here, and when you read the Qur'an and you understand that you're talking to God and these are God's words, and if you understand what's written in the Qur'an, you won't need to go to any Masjid or any Imam...
>
> *(Shukri from Syria, quoted in Pertek, 2022a:233)*

Most of the women said they drew incredible strength from their religion and managed their stress with the help of their religion, known as religious coping (Pargament, 1997). While religious coping is known to modify emotions (Lazarus and Folkman, 1984), overall emotional focused coping is considered less helpful in finding solutions than problem-focused coping (Zakar et al., 2012). Some may argue that religious coping tactics, as dominantly emotion-focused, deprive women of agency because it facilitates them staying in violent relationships. In fact, I argue the opposite. Reflecting on the lived experiences of the women I interacted with, religious coping was to them an agential act of co-opting with God to actively seek to change their situations. Finding strength in religion was an agentic act of survivors, often in powerless situations, seeking to change their situations, using resources (e.g. supernatural power) within their reach and control. Within their religious belief systems, they believed the power of God was able to change their circumstances, and this is the power they called on. Many respondents felt that their prayers, answered by God in some ways, manifested in positive life changes. While it is true that some displaced survivors, in extremely precarious circumstances, did not have access to other avenues to bring change, simply dismissing survivors' religious coping resources would mean undermining their strengths and what mattered for them during their hardship. It would also mean not supporting their coping mechanisms. Moreover, claiming that religious coping in response to VAWG experiences is a passive response (rather than an act of agency) is an act of epistemic violence against survivors, for their worldviews are questioned from the perspective of an outsider's worldviews. In my study, religious coping was crucial for psychological survival of religious women survivors and deeply related to their immense personal strength, too (Pertek, 2022a, 2022b).

There is plenty of evidence demonstrating an association between patterns of religious coping, based on religious beliefs and practices, and mental health constructs. For instance, the fact that many respondents in my research experienced feelings of safety due to their relationship with God corresponds to the claim that the perception of divine control (i.e. the belief that God controls the course of one's life) is reported to have a strong association with positive psychological reappraisal coping, buffering the adverse effects of traumatic events of individuals (DeAngelis and Ellison, 2017).

Religious experience: From empowerment and survival to healing

With the survivors from Syria and Iraq interviewed in Turkey, their religious ideas and practices manifested in lived religious/spiritual experiences. Holding tight to religious ideas and intense religious practices led some survivors to undergoing deep religious and spiritual experiences. These experiences manifested in certain attitudes, moods and motivations, enhancing their coping with exploitation and sometimes encouraging inner transformation, such as mobilising strength to leave abusive relationships. Such experiences arguably also prevented survivors/victims from more serious mental health conditions. Subjective religious experiences – spiritual events, feelings and emotions – shaped respondents' lives through night-time dreams, the realisation of prayers and sensing God's presence before and during forced migration.

Some of the women, I interviewed, reflected on spiritual experiences of survival. Recalling the Qur'an or Bible and praying shaped their spiritual experiences in which they felt God's 'touch' and 'protection' in their lives. This, in turn, deepened their faith. Experiences of safety or survival not only strengthened their faith but also were often described as religious experiences in itself. Through their religious belief, trust in God and envisioning escape and survival, respondents found 'power within' which they attributed to their faith. As religious beliefs and practices made them stronger, a faith-inspired 'power within' grew that was often mentioned in relation to their inner strength:

> It's in the Mediterranean Sea that I saw people drowning, I am not a good swimmer, but that day I had the strength to swim and to even save another life. Right in front of me I saw people going down and never showing up again…God has a reason for me to be alive…he is the reason why I am alive, actually my religion got more stronger because I am not scared of death, when it comes, I know I have to go, but God gave me another chance to live, so this made stronger connection with him…
>
> *(Ayesha from Sierra Leone, interview in 2019)*

Women's continued prayers and invocations shaped their religious experiences by engaging their emotions and feelings which often led to uplifting their spirits and creating sense of safety beyond material reality. Many respondents felt God's protection during life-threatening situations. African survivors described feeling safeguarded by God (in response to their prayers) from kidnapping, sex trafficking and detention (Pertek, 2022b), while Levantine survivors talked of being shielded from war violence, atrocities, honour-based violence, domestic violence and sexual exploitation (Pertek, 2022a).

For many, VAWG experience took on a spiritual meaning-making and itself became part of religious experience, in which survivors' thinking framework centred on the connection with God and the invisible powers. Deep existential meaning-making made them interpret their worldly hardship as part of religious experience which would admit them to heaven. In practice spiritual meaning-making allowed them to positively reappraise their stressors and resist hardship. For instance, a Syrian religious survivor residing in Turkey rejected transactional sex offers in exchange for money based on *hadiths* promising paradise for those resisting illicit sexual relations:

> Seven shall be shaded by Allah under his shade on a Day [of Judgment] in which there is no shade except His Shade…a man [woman] invited by a woman [man] of status and beauty, but he says: 'I fear Allah, Mighty and Sublime is He'…
>
> *(Mira from Syria, citing a hadith narrated by Abu Hurairah[1], Pertek, 2022a:228)*

Second, most respondents came to terms with the situations they were facing through the patience and inner strength they derived from their faith. Three of the survivors interviewed in Turkey explained that the faith-inspired patience and acceptance were what prevented them from committing suicide. These women interpreted their experiences as God testing their patience, and with the desire to be found worthy and good, they restrained from taking their lives. Among the women I met, many lost close family members, including their own children. One of them, Kameela, lost her son in the 'Bakery Massacre' (bombardment on Aleppo), and before that had lost her brother and father. Her spirituality soothed her pain and enabled her to continue her life in faith:

> From Allah, he granted me patience. I lost my son, so if it wasn't for Allah's help, I'd have broken down and given up… When my son died, I thought I'd commit suicide, but Allah gave me peace of mind, and prayer and Qur'an helped me become more patient. After I buried my son, I looked up and cried that Allah grants me patience…If Allah hadn't granted me patience, I'd have cried every time I looked at my son's photos…but now…I speak about him proudly, thanks to Allah.
>
> *(Kameela from Syria, quoted in Pertek, 2022a:238)*

For some respondents, profound religious supplications (invocations to God) and framing their personal experiences within religious narratives known from religious scriptures, supported healing from severe psychological distress. Spiritual experiences, such as feelings of empowerment, often reframed survivors' cognitive processes and activated positive emotions in them, such as feelings of peace. Women often talked to God and those who were literate usually read the religious texts too to engage with divine guidance. Many were inspired by stories of their role models (i.e. their Prophets and other key figures) in the Qur'an. Night-time dreams carried different meanings and symbols in their lives and were often interpreted by several survivors as signs from God that gave them courage. For one survivor reading the Qur'an served as a timekeeper for her forthcoming divorce, requesting God that by the time she finishes to read the entire script, she would be already divorced. Such an action operated as a claim on God and an act of belief that brought her resilience. She compared her divorce to, and drew strength from, one of the chapters of the Qur'an:

> I read the Qur'an a lot, and patience, I had no doubt that I could be strong to leave my husband. Sometimes, I see my

divorce like Surah [chapter] Youssef; it started with a dream, a vision, and ended with reality.

(Shukri from Syria, quoted in Pertek, 2022a:228)

Hypothetically spiritual experiences can also impact perpetrators' attitudes, who may find in their spiritual beliefs an explanation for conflict in their relationships, which may be useful for preventing and responding to VAWG. Anecdotally, for instance, if a perpetrator finds that marital discord is a result of interference from the invisible (spiritual) world (e.g. spells, evil eye and black magic), he may believe that exorcism (removing evil spirits or 'jinns') can help address and manage potential tension points that lead to violence. A wife's disobedience may be seen as spiritual possession which requires interventions to support healing and reconciliation. When seeking alternative religious healing practices, one such practice is *ruqayyah* – a cure method based on the power of the Qur'an recited by religious leaders and traditional healers – which victims and perpetrators may apply in order to remove spirit possession of affected individual and alleviate family conflict. Such religious healing methods rely on the healing from the invisible world by reciting the verses from the Qur'an and was reported in use in various settings, for example, among Rohingya refugees (Tay et al., 2018). Religious healing methods play a significant role in treating mental health conditions in the Muslim world. Further research should explore the role of religious/spiritual experiences in VAWG perpetration and prevention and seek to understand traditional and religious help-seeking behaviours and healing practices. This is needed to inform development of culturally and faith-sensitive psycho-social support and treatment for religious populations.

Religious organisation: Mobilising policy for faith anti-VAWG practice

In this section, I explore how religious organisation can be crucial to opposing VAWG by drawing on work I conducted as a gender practitioner with Islamic Relief Worldwide (IRW), and in collaboration with Islamic Relief Ethiopia (IRE). I argue that religious organisations and communities can mobilise to oppose VAWG by leveraging their religious ideas. The communal dimension of religion allows people to organise themselves on the basis of their belief – and I argue that this organisation can be directed against VAWG. Below, I first explore the IRW's faith-sensitive integration of gender into its policy and programmes, followed by an exploration of programmatic examples from IRE enabled by IRW's policy.

A crucial component of the anti-VAWG communal organisation by IRW was the Qur'an, which is a source of guidance in Muslim communities. As a text with authority, the Qur'an remains an important resource which can operate as a foundation for organisational policy development in faith communities. Such process somehow manifested in case of IRW and its global federation in around 40 countries where faith-based imperatives encouraged action for the protection of women and girls. First, in mobilising to oppose VAWG, IRW developed a comprehensive gender policy which encouraged its national offices to develop faith-sensitive VAWG programmes. The global Gender Justice Policy (the development and implementation of which I led between 2014 and 2018) clearly was anchored in the religious values of the organisation, but had a practical imperative to meet humanitarian standards and commitment to Sustainable Development Goal (SDG) 5 to 'achieve gender equality and empower all women and girls'. This policy drew upon an understanding of gender equality that combined Islamic and secular human rights perspectives.

While many consider gender justice as compatible with the Islamic tradition (Carland, 2017; Chaudhry, 2017), some critics may argue the opposite. Yet, IRW's policy makes an organisational commitment to draw upon Islamic teachings for condemning VAWG and dismantling misconceptions around spousal discipline and harmful practices (IRW, 2015). In the process of developing the IRW's Gender Justice Policy, three principles enshrined in the Qur'an served as reference points: dignity (Qur'an 17:70[2]), equality before God (Qur'an 4:1[3]; 49:13) and justice in social relations, rights and responsibilities (Qur'an 4:135; 5:8; 16:90). Besides, the international human rights instruments, the policy also mentioned some faith references to women's rights, such as access to resources and education (Qur'an 96:1–5), distribution of inheritance (Qur'an 4:7), property and land rights (Qur'an 4:29), control over earnings and right to work. In addition, it built on faith traditions that encourage fairness in treatment, care and empowerment of women, for example, partly drawing upon the Qur'an's chapter dedicated to women (Chapter 4, '*al-Nisa*', 'Women'), which calls for unconditional justice: "You who believe, uphold justice and bear witness to God, even if it is against yourselves, your parents, or your close relatives" (Qur'an 4:135). In addition, IRW's Gender Justice Policy leveraged Prophet Muhammed's (PBUH) narrations to protect women's rights, emphasising the equal value of women, for example, drawing on the *hadith* narrated by imam Abu-Dawood: "Assuredly, women are the twin halves of men".

Since the adoption of the gender policy, IRW embarked on various initiatives to promote gender justice and end VAWG. This included efforts to develop an Islamic Declaration on Gender Justice (Ashraf and Abukar, 2020), integrated GBV and Child Protection programme (Pertek et al., 2020), joint Channels of Hope programmes with World Vision (see Le Roux, this volume) and IRE's VAWG project (2016–2017). It is this IRE VAWG project that serves as a further illustration of how religious organisation can address VAWG, demonstrating how religious communities can organise themselves to counter it.

In 2016–2017, IRE implemented a VAWG pilot project entitled 'Combating Gender-Based Violence of Women and Girls in the Dekasuftu Woreda of Liben Zone' in the Somali region of Ethiopia. The project was developed based on the findings of a gender assessment, which I coordinated during IRW's gender policy development (some findings of which I have outlined in Chapter 4). This pilot project used a community conversation approach and aimed to (a) engage religious leaders in combating discriminatory norms and decreasing tolerance of VAWG, (b) increase safety of women and girls and (c) promote access to health services for survivors. First, IRE organised theological and human rights training for local religious leaders from the remote areas of Dekasuftu Woreda. Upon their return to their villages, these leaders, together with community volunteers, recruited and trained by IRE, worked to challenge harmful practices and discriminatory attitudes towards women and girls in their communities, by clarifying religious and cultural misconceptions.

A key component of religious leaders' and volunteers' engagement on VAWG in their communities was through facilitated, single-sex and mixed conversation groups. One of the central issues discussed in women's and men's community conversations was domestic violence. To challenge dominant attitudes in local communities that condone and tolerate domestic violence, religious leaders developed Friday sermons to share religious teachings on non-violence and women's rights in the family, encouraging their congregations to restrain from inflicting harm. They, alongside the volunteers, used an Islamic perspective to condemn spousal violence and rape by referencing the Qur'an and the *hadiths* (Prophetic narrations) and emphasised the Islamic traditions of honouring and treating women kindly. For example, they recalled: "The best of you are those who are the best to their wives, and I am the best of you to my wives" (Prophet Muhammed narrated by Sunan Ibn Majah). This very same teaching was mentioned by Sara from Syria (earlier in this Chapter).

In line with the Islamic pro-women ethos, some community members during community conversations stated that women had equal or superior rights to men, referring to the position of a mother in the family. The religious concept which assigns a triple priority of mothers over fathers, as coined by Prophet Muhammed in a *hadith*, served as a key argument in conversations on protecting women's status and interests. This *hadith* explicitly discussed the importance of mothers:

> A man came to the Prophet and said, 'O Messenger of God! Who among the people is the most worthy of my good companionship? The Prophet said: Your mother. The man said, 'Then who?' The Prophet said: Then your mother. The man further asked, 'Then who?' The Prophet said: Then your mother. The man asked again, 'Then who?' The Prophet said: Then your father. (Prophet Muhammed narrated by Imam Al-Bukhari and Imam Muslim, Hadith no. 316, An-Nawawi, 1999)

Faith-inspired anti-VAWG messaging was accompanied by a range of behavioural change communication methods to raise public awareness, including dedicated discussions in school clubs and community role-plays. As a result, the community observed increased reporting of violent incidents and women claiming their social and economic rights, such as the right to dowry:

> Previously before the intervention if a marriage gift (mahr) is given to a woman during her marriage lifetime we used to perceive it as a divorce (or sign of it). After the intervention we have learned that marriage gift (mahr) and divorce are not related; and we start to request or accept our mahr at any time.
>
> *(Amina, a female group representative, Sero Kebele, IRE quoted in Pertek, 2020:144)*

Women, some of whom previously used to tolerate abuse, were reported by IRE to start opposing VAWG, declaring their determination to combat misconceptions and tolerance of domestic violence locally. IRE reported that male group members participating in the community conversations also condemned spousal violence and promised to restrain and raise awareness of others (Pertek, 2020).

Finally, drawing on the religious traditions, some myths concerning violence against women and girls were dismantled in local community and helped several participants reclaim their dowry rights, report abuse and enter education (ibid.). One of the myths dismantled by religious leaders was the belief in 'marriage by inheritance' (Chapter 4), a form of socio-cultural violence enforced upon widowed women, where they are forced to marry their deceased husband's brother. During community conversations, religious leaders tackled such beliefs from a religious perspective, explaining that Islam did not allow such marriages. Another practice challenged was female genital mutilation and/or cutting (FGM/C), through raising awareness of the associated health harms and by discussing the *hadiths* opposing the cutting of female genitals. Upon realising FGM/C was a sinful act, dissociated from Islam (Lethome Asmani and Abdi, 2008) and against Islamic teachings, women and FGM/C practitioners cried and sought repentance from God.

Women FGM/C practitioners also questioned why previous religious leaders did not tell them that FGM/C is a forbidden act. Local women, including FGM/C practitioners, declared that they will seek to stop FGM/C in their communities and requested training sessions that will enable them to develop grassroots advocacy capacities. According to IRE reports, the local branch recorded a gradual shift from the severest forms of FGM/C to a complete FGM/C rejection by some practitioners (ibid).

In sum, IRW's and IRE's examples illustrate how religious organisations can be crucial to countering VAWG due to their policies and programmes. In their experience, integrating humanitarian and faith-based discourses produced quite unexpected avenues for promoting gender justice and upholding women's rights in local religious communities in ways that were contextually sensitive and arguably more impactful. The case study of Islamic Relief shows that gender policies in FBOs that are grounded in their inherent beliefs and traditions of justice can bring about positive change. The IRE case study also shows the power and potentials of religious organisations to organise on the basis of their belief in effective ways countering VAWG, through mobilising faith-inspired policy and practice.

Conclusion

Religion can operate as a protective resource in VAWG. Religious resources can provide survivors with intellectual and spiritual tools to buffer the effects of VAWG, while the Qur'an as a source of guidance and authority to transform the way religious organisations operate. I identified a range of functions of religion from meaning-making (religious ideas), coping (religious practices), empowerment and healing (religious experiences) and faith-sensitive organisation of communities. Overall the chapter demonstrates that leveraging religious resources can mobilise resistance against VAWG among survivors and from within religious organisations. Findings point to the importance of adapting a faith-sensitive approach to working with religious survivors and religious communities and a continued engagement with religious factors in the intersection with cultural and socio-economic factors. IRE's project demonstrates how faith communities can organise to counter VAWG based on their religious beliefs and religious practices by engaging with the religion and culture nexus which may engender vulnerability (as discussed in Chapter 4) but also create space for positive social change.

The above findings also highlight the importance of recognising and supporting religious coping strategies among survivors and victims of VAWG to help facilitate their healing. A holistic support includes recognising impact of religious coping on the wellbeing of survivors and helping to resolve spiritual struggles which may undermine recovery. Moreover, religious experiences, rarely considered in VAWG interventions, have profound implications on violence prevention and response and need better integration into interventions. Subjective experiences of religion are deeply personal expressions and observations of the inner and outer world, inspired by invisible world, which profoundly intricate with mental health of religious survivors. Effective responses would require to engage with the religious thinking frameworks of survivors and perpetrators to rupture VAWG effectively.

Notes

1 Abu Hurairah (Abdur-Rahman ibn Sakhr Al-Dawsi Al-Zahrani) was one of the companions of Prophet Muhammed.
2 All Qur'anic quotations used in this chapter refer to Abdullah Yusuf Ali (2013) translations.
3 "People, be mindful of your Lord, who created you from a single soul, and from it created its mate, and from the pair of them spread countless men and women far and wide…" (Qur'an, 4:1).

References

Ahmed, L. (1992). *Women and gender in Islam: Historical roots of a modern debate*. New Haven, CT: Yale University Press.

An-Nawawi, Y. (1999). *Commentary on the Riyad-us-Saliheen*. Vol. 1. Riyadh: Darussalam, 295.

Ashraf, S. and Abukar, N. (2020). "Gender and Islam", in A.A. Khan and A. Cheema (eds.), *Islam and International Development: Insights for working with Muslim communities*. Rugby, UK: Practical Action Publishing, 111–129.

Ashrof, V.A.M. (2005). *Islam and gender justice*. Delhi: Kalpaz Publications.

Carland, S. (2017). "Islam and feminism are not mutually exclusive, and faith can be an important liberator." *The Conversation* (10 May). Viewed from https://theconversation.com/islam-and-feminism-are-not-mutually-exclusive-and-faith-can-be-an-important-liberator-77086.

Chaudhry, A.S. (2013). *Domestic violence and the Islamic tradition*. Oxford, UK: Oxford University Press.

DeAngelis, R. and Ellison, C. (2017). "Kept in his care: The role of perceived divine control in positive reappraisal coping", *Religions*, 8. doi:10.3390/rel8080133.

Ghafournia, N. (2017). "Muslim women and domestic violence: Developing a framework for social work practice", *Journal of Religion & Spirituality in Social Work: Social Thought*, 36(1–2): 146–163. doi:10.1080/15426432.2017.1313150.

Hassouneh-Phillips, D. (2003). "Strength and vulnerability: Spirituality in abused American Muslim women's lives", *Issues in Mental Health Nursing*, 24 (6–7): 681–694. doi:10.1080/01612840305324.

IRW (2015). *Gender justice policy*. Birmingham: Islamic Relief Worldwide.

Lazarus, R.S. and Folkman, S. (1984). *Stress, appraisal, and coping*. New York: Springer Publishing Company.

Lethome Asmani, I. and Abdi, M. (2008). *Delinking female genital mutilation/cutting from Islam*. Population Council. doi:10.31899/rh14.1025.

Mernissi, F. (1991). *The veil and the male elite: A feminist interpretation of women's rights in Islam*. New York, NY: Addison-Wesley.

Minganti, P.K. (2015). "Muslim women managing women's shelters: Somaya, the Muslimwoman and religion as resource", *NORA - Nordic Journal of Feminist and Gender Research*, 23(2): 93–108. doi:10.1080/08038740.2014.935744.

Mir-Hosseini, Z. (2006). "Muslim women's quest for equality: Between Islamic law and feminism", *Critical Inquiry*, 32: 629–645.

Pargament, K.I. (1997). *The psychology of religion and coping*. New York, NY: Guilford Press.

Pertek, S.I. (2020). "Deconstructing Islamic perspectives on sexual and gender-based violence, toward a faith inclusive approach", in A.A. Khan and A. Cheema (eds.), *Islam and International Development: Insights for working with Muslim communities*. Rugby, UK: Practical Action Publishing, 131–152.

Pertek, S.I. (2022a). "Religion, forced migration and the continuum of violence: An intersectional and ecological analysis", PhD Dissertation, University of Birmingham.

Pertek, S.I. (2022b). "'God helped us': Resilience, religion and experiences of gender-based violence and trafficking among African forced migrant women", *Social Sciences*, 11(5): 201. doi:10.3390/socsci11050201.

Pertek, S.I., Almugahed, N. and Fida, N. (2020). "Integrating gender-based violence and child protection, an exploration of Islamic Relief's approaches", in K. Kraft and O.J. Wilkinson (eds.), *International development and local faith actors: Ideological and cultural encounters*. Oxon, New York, NY: Routledge, 108–121.

Qur'an (2013). Translated by Abdullah Yusuf Ali. Ware, Hertfordshire: Wordsworth Editions Limited.

Rutledge, K., Pertek, S., Abo-Hilal, M. and Fitzgibbon, A. (2021) "Faith and mental health and psycho-social support among displaced Muslim women", *Forced Migration Review*, 66.

Tay, A.K., Islam, R., Riley, A., Welton-Mitchell, C., Duchesne, B., Waters, V., Varner, A., Silove, D. and Ventevogel, P. (2018). *Culture, context and mental health of Rohingya refugees: A review for staff in mental health and psychosocial support programmes for Rohingya refugees*. Geneva: UNHCR. Viewed from https://www.unhcr.org/5bbc6f014.pdf [Date accessed: February 15, 2021].

Wadud, A. (2006). *Inside the gender Jihad: Women's reform in Islam*. Oxford, UK: Oneworld Publications.

Zakar, R., Zakar, M.Z. and Krämer, A. (2012). "Voices of strength and struggle: Women's coping strategies against spousal violence in Pakistan", *Journal of Interpersonal Violence*, 27(16): 3268–3298. doi:10.1177/0886260512441257.

9

JOINT REFLECTIONS ON RELIGION COUNTERING VIOLENCE AGAINST WOMEN AND GIRLS

Elisabet le Roux and Sandra Iman Pertek

The preceding two chapters explored how two religions, Christianity and Islam, are contributing positively to preventing violence against women and girls (VAWG) and responding to it. Relying on findings and case studies from various studies conducted by the authors in different countries, and on the analysis of literature relevant in the field, the chapters offered a rich reflection on the potentially positive contribution of religion to addressing VAWG. Here we use these chapters as the starting point for a more general reflection on the positive contribution of religion to VAWG prevention and response.

First, we recognise the potential of a scriptural approach to resisting VAWG. Both Christianity and Islam have a central sacred text and rich narrative tradition with much authority. This can be leveraged for VAWG prevention and response in different ways, for example, by promoting scriptures and interpretations that call for non-violence and gender equality. A scriptural approach aims for social transformation through re-interpreting scriptures and countering interpretations that lead to gender inequality and VAWG, using scriptures that discuss VAWG to counter the taboo

DOI: 10.4324/9781003169086-12

on speaking out about VAWG and relying on sacred texts' call to charity and support for the oppressed as a motivation for care for survivors.

The challenge is that re-interpretations of scriptures can always be countered by others who offer opposing interpretations. This risk points to the need, especially with religious leaders, to not only offer specific re-interpretations of scripture but to also capacitate the individual to reflect and engage with the sacred texts which matter to them. Many religious leaders (at different levels of the religious hierarchy) have had little or no theological training and/ or are often only exposed to the teachings of conservative groups. Therefore, interventions that not simply enforce new ways of reading scriptures, but actually capacitate the individual to be able to read and interpret sacred scriptures in light of wider religious ethics and hermeneutics, is an important step. If a person of faith is only convinced of the importance of gender equality and non-violence based on a certain interpretation of scripture promoted by another person, and not based on their personal engagement with and understanding of sacred scriptures, it is easier for them to be swayed again. What is called for here is a kind of personal transformation, where the individual is internalising alternative interpretations of sacred text and how it applies to contemporary life.

This leads to a recognition of the important role of religious actors, not only as the target group of interventions, but as implementers and partners in VAWG interventions. It requires a person that knows the religion and sacred scriptures well, and has the authority to speak on and about it, to engage and guide other people of faith in such a journey of personal, alternative engagement with sacred scriptures. Secular development organisations and practitioners do not have the knowledge, skill or authority to do so.

Engaging with religion and religious actors, especially when using a scriptural approach, often requires significant theological resources. In this regard, faith-based organisations (FBOs) potentially have a unique contribution to make. Especially larger FBOs may have the staff and resources to develop the needed theological resources, which can then in turn be used by local religious actors. In the case of interfaith efforts, FBOs may be better positioned to collaborate and develop the needed materials. As was illustrated in the examples from Islamic Relief Worldwide in Chapter 8 and World Vision and Islamic Relief Worldwide in Chapter 7, considerable time, effort and money go into engaging with sacred scripture on gender equality and non-violence. If such theological resources can be developed by FBOs, they can be used widely with and by local religious actors. Such partnerships can be especially valuable for international FBOs, who do not (necessarily) have relationships and trust at local level. By developing tools and offering support, they can capacitate the local religious actors that are better positioned to mobilise communities around re-interpretations of sacred text and transformation of religious practices at local level.

We also see that engaging around sacred scriptures can potentially be a meeting point for interfaith collaboration on addressing VAWG. Where people of different religions have a sacred scripture in common, or where there is respect for all sacred scriptures, there is potential for such collaboration, which can in turn contribute to interreligious cohesion and cooperation. Such interfaith collaboration contributes to recognising VAWG as a common, community-wide problem, rather than a secret, taboo issue that must be kept quiet or blamed on the religious other. A community-wide attempt to address VAWG has a much better chance of succeeding in changing the dominant norms and practices within the community. The feasibility of such interfaith engagement around sacred scripture will depend on the setting and will be exceedingly challenging where there is already interreligious distrust and conflict. For example, such an approach may work in South Africa or Senegal, but arguably not in Nigeria or Pakistan.

What we also see illustrated in the preceding two chapters is that sacred scripture can empower women, including survivors. Through individual reading, listening to and even re-interpreting sacred scriptures, women find the strength and motivation to resist and overcome harmful and violent circumstances. Using a scripture can be an act of empowerment, where the survivor claims the right to read and interpret it as a life-saving, violence-resisting text that prioritises women's safety. For victims who are unable to leave violent relationships, such use of scriptures may even be their only weapon or act of resistance, yet one that strengthens them and offers them refuge. The case studies in the preceding chapters counter the common belief that sacred scriptures necessarily subjugate and disempower women, due to the patriarchal norms and beliefs propagated in these religious texts. As presented in Chapter 8, women drew immense strength from their engagement with religious texts to cope with violence and displacement. Women can also, through the reading and claiming of certain scriptures, use and experience these scriptures as empowering and liberating. In some cases, it may mean that some women intentionally move away from institutional religion, finding its application as patriarchal and misused to justify VAWG. In other settings, such individualised religious practices may develop as circumstances prohibit engagement with institutional religion (e.g. when a survivor loses touch with her religious community during forced migration).

Religious coping is often dismissed as depriving women of agency or an avoidance of personal responsibility by delegating it to a divine figure. Yet the preceding chapters have explored the importance of religious coping as an agential act by survivors and women at risk of violence. In a situation of great powerlessness, these women seek to change their circumstances through their relationship with their God. By using religious resources such as prayer, fasting or scripture reading, these women actively seek to change their circumstances. For these women, religious coping is a powerful and even political act which does not require institutional religion, thus holding the potential for revolutionary change at an individual level. Such personal engagement with religion highlights the importance of VAWG interventions that work directly with religious women, creating and allowing safe spaces for them to discuss religious matters and drawing on their (and not necessarily on institutional) religious perspectives.

Reflecting on how religious women experience their religion in challenging circumstances, including when experiencing VAWG, emphasises that the international development sector has to stop dismissing the role and impact of religious experiences. The impact of experiences such as prayer, dreams and faith healing is easily dismissed as esoteric, unreal or imagined. However, the experiences of especially survivors show us that these are critically important resources for religious women, especially in providing mental health and psycho-social support and when working on the healing, reintegration and resilience-building of survivors. Ignoring religious experiences means ignoring a potentially impactful resource for VAWG prevention and response.

The preceding two chapters have also highlighted the importance of respecting and responding to context when engaging religion and religious actors around VAWG prevention and response. The beliefs, norms and practices that can be leveraged for non-violence and gender equality are distinct to each community and depend on context, as do the harmful beliefs, norms and practices that need to be addressed. Practitioners working to end VAWG will need to explore and understand the varying nature and roles of religious resources *within their specific context* and engage appropriately. For example, the language and terminology used when engaging on VAWG will need to be appropriate to the context and will require piloting and testing with communities, taking into account how religious norms inform local terminologies being used. It may even require rethinking terms that have negative associations in that particular setting, such as 'gender equality' or 'women's rights'. The aim is to find the entry points and framing that invite religious actors and communities to support non-violence and gender equality, allowing them to use their religious resources and integrate their worldview sensitively for joint collaboration and partnership on an equal footing.

The importance of respecting context challenges international development actors to embrace comprehensive conceptualisations of religious literacy. Those who wish to engage with religion and religious actors on VAWG need to know and understand more than only the basic tenets of the specific religion. They need to understand the different and changing religious beliefs, norms and practices in the specific setting and how these generally impact the wider community, but also specifically VAWG in the domestic and public spheres. When striving to develop such an understanding, it is important to be mindful of where such insight and knowledge is found. Informants of various social backgrounds (e.g. in terms of gender, class, race and sects) with different perspectives will offer a more balanced account of local religious practices and beliefs. In addition, learning about the egalitarian principles and interpretations of religious texts can be important entry points to help forge meaningful relationships with religious actors and develop faith-sensitive VAWG programming. Furthermore, engagement with formal and informal organisations of women of faith can be particularly insightful in the process of recognising existing local resources and actors to address VAWG.

The role, authority, influence and importance of religious leaders in addressing VAWG has been highlighted. They are a critical dimension of working with religion and religious communities and serve as gatekeepers to religious communities. In many religious groups, especially ones with strict hierarchical structures, it is impossible to engage with religious communities without going through their leaders. Their support for VAWG interventions and the messaging of such interventions are often critical to its success. At the same time, the reality is that religious leaders are most often men. Yet, when working on VAWG, the inclusion of the voices and leadership of women is paramount. If only male religious leaders represent a religious community and mediate between the community and outsiders, this means that, once again, only male perspectives are represented. This can lead to women's rights and needs being ignored. Such 'unintentional' exclusion highlights the need to be intentional, strategic and creative to also identify and work with women religious leaders. In many religious communities, this may mean engaging with informal religious leadership and women's groups.

Ultimately, what we see when reflecting on the two preceding chapters as a whole is that religion and religious actors carry great potential and resources for contributing to VAWG prevention and response. Due to the various religious resources that are uniquely connected to religion, religion potentially offers a unique and much-needed contribution to VAWG prevention and response. But for this potential to be leveraged and form part of holistic efforts to address VAWG, the international development community has to be open to recognising and acknowledging the extensive resources that religion has, and the unique contributions it can make to VAWG prevention and response, in parallel to existing anti-VAWG efforts. Especially in terms of religious experiences, there is often a hesitancy to recognise the impact they have, and therefore the value of religion is excluded in the design and implementation of VAWG interventions, ignoring the lived realities of many survivors. A key prerequisite for fully engaging religious resources for VAWG prevention and responses is for the international development community to recognise their potential as assets and develop adequate capacities for constructive engagement and integration to end VAWG.

PART IV

Looking to the future

10

NOW WHAT? IMPLICATIONS FOR RESEARCHERS, POLICYMAKERS AND PRACTITIONERS

Sandra Iman Pertek and Elisabet le Roux

In writing this book, our aim was to identify and unpack how religion and religious actors contribute to the continued perpetration of violence against women and girls (VAWG) as well as how they contribute to the prevention of and response to it. Seeking a balanced and nuanced account, we explored both Christian and Muslim settings to better understand the intersections between religion and VAWG. Our research in many different contexts with high religiosity and fragility have highlighted that building on the positive contributions of religion and religious actors can be significant and valuable to anti-VAWG efforts. At the same time, the importance of addressing the negative roles and influences of religion and religious actors has also come to the fore.

We followed Ter Haar's (2011) framework of religious resources in structuring this book. On the whole, it is fair to say the framework worked well for the purposes of organising the book. While we used the framework as a heuristic tool, we realise that using a framework in the analysis of religion runs the risk of dictating or dominating how religion is understood and presented, and not necessarily representing the complex reality. In real life, religious

DOI: 10.4324/9781003169086-14

resources may overlap and the boundaries between them may be blurred. Using religious resources as a framework, therefore, should be done with caution so as to ensure that the analysis remains true and representative of the different meanings of religion among diverse social groups.

Building on the empirical and reflection chapters in Parts II and III, we now consider what this means for policymakers, practitioners and researchers involved in addressing and studying VAWG. Simply put, Religion Matters! The VAWG sector should take religion into account. Engagement on VAWG is insufficient if it does not do so, for ignoring or avoiding religion means ignoring or avoiding a dimension of both individual and communal life that plays a fundamental role in how the majority of the global population perceive gender equality, VAWG and what should be done about these.

In striving to support a VAWG sector that is able to engage with religion, we have identified seven key implications of the intersection between religion and VAWG that are essential for strengthening VAWG prevention and response. This chapter shares these implications, offering pragmatic and change-oriented recommendations for researchers, policymakers and practitioners.

Implication 1: Engage religious resources and religious actors in VAWG

For most of the global population, religion remains a part of their communities' social fabric and dictates or influences gender dynamics. It carries meaningful social, psychological and material resources which can be leveraged for VAWG prevention and response. Recognising the powerful potential of religious actors and religious resources for addressing VAWG and supporting survivors' healing is the first step towards meaningfully engaging with religion in anti-VAWG efforts. Religious resources can enable religious actors to join efforts to address VAWG, as it allows them to align such efforts with their worldview. For those who are religious, anti-VAWG efforts that resonate with their worldview and speak the language of religion can be more effective in stimulating reflection on VAWG compared to interventions that use only foreign concepts originating from value systems outside of their cosmological order.

At the same time, drawing on religion and religious actors in programming to address VAWG runs the risk of instrumentalising religion to advance programmatic agendas. Intentional effort should be put into avoiding such instrumentalisation. This can be done by facilitating dialogue and engagement and building equitable partnerships with religious actors (individual, communal and institutional) and learning from them about the religious traditions, concepts and practices which they can engage to counter VAWG. Such processes of engagement require open-mindedness to discover local ways of looking at VAWG prevention and responses, appreciating the wealth of local knowledge among religious actors. Such engagement may require secular and religious outsiders to step outside of their comfort zone in order to be able to discover the traditions and religious resources that have the potential to reduce violence and build resilience. If such time and effort is invested, the anti-VAWG perspectives that are often inherently present in their understanding of religion can be identified and engaged. For example, many religious traditions emphasise the importance of preserving human dignity, human rights and promoting peace in family and local communities, and this is a religious principle that can be mobilised in anti-VAWG efforts.

Implication 2: Recognise the role and potential of religious experiences

Religious experiences refer to the metaphysical attitudes, moods and motivations that religion may incite in believers, for example, experiences of inner transformation, healing and empowerment. The religious experiences of women and survivors can contribute to or challenge VAWG. Engaging with religion in VAWG interventions requires taking the religious experiences of women and survivors into account because these experiences often constitute VAWG experience. As illustrated in Parts II and III, religious experiences can contribute to continued victimisation, but also lead to survivors resisting or escaping violent situations. Especially VAWG interventions that address the mental health of victims and survivors need to consider how religious experiences may influence the implementation of their programmes. Psychological, emotional and spiritual well-being are related (Williamson and Robinson, 2006), and therefore religious experiences should be taken into account in programmes that engage with religious survivors. A holistic response to survivors' well-being is required to cater for survivors' multi-dimensional needs where lived experiences of religion, shaping mental health conditions and practical outcomes, are understood and engaged with.

Implication 3: Recognise the agency of religious women survivors

The agency of religious women, including religious women survivors, need to be recognised. While religious survivors' reliance on religious beliefs and practices may seem to be only passive coping strategies, the automatic assumption should not be that they are victims of religion. When religious women's obedience to religious precepts are instinctively dismissed as non-agentic, it leads to patronising and infantilising attitudes towards religious women, which in turn undermine these women's recovery and strength.

Instead of assuming their lack of agency, we should question our core assumptions about survivors' coping, acknowledging that (as an outsider) we may misunderstand their lived experiences of religion. As was explored in Part 3, survivors' reliance on religion is very often an intentional act of agency and even defiance through which they resist the violence that is perpetrated against them and the ways in which it is justified. While it does not always (or immediately) lead to a woman leaving a violent situation, there is nevertheless agency in how she engages with religion.

Certainly, not all actions of all religious women at all times are indications of agency. But the default assumption should not be that religious survivors passively allow their victimisation by using religion to cope with it. Debilitating and reductionist assumptions concerning religious women's agency should be avoided, and instead the default position should be to identify and recognise their acts of agency and to acknowledge and support them where their recovery is facilitated by the reliance on the religious resources that matter to them the most.

Implication 4: Engage with religion when working with perpetrators who are religious

When working with perpetrators who are religious, interventions should also draw on perpetrators' religious beliefs, as religion influences such perpetrators' attitudes and behaviours. While there are existing programmes that work with men and boys using a religious lens, there is a dearth of programmes that works specifically with perpetrators using a religious lens. This means the potential of drawing on perpetrators' religious ideas, practices and experiences remains untapped. For example, prayers and religious ceremonies, which provide psycho-social support, stress reduction and healing, may help some perpetrators manage anger and other difficult emotions, dissuading from escalating violence. Another potential avenue is drawing on religious texts to argue against VAWG and promote women's rights and familial harmony. Interventions that focus on anger management and communication skills can link these with religious traditions and ethics.

Although incorporating faith perspectives in working with perpetrators who are religious could tap into creative pathways of reforming perpetrators, it is important to emphasise that not all perpetrators are actually religious, even though they may identify with a certain religion. As explored in Chapters 4 and 8, perpetrators may associate with a religious community, yet not actually practice the religion. With such perpetrators, religion-based/ inspired programmes may be unsuitable.

Implication 5: Prioritise religious literacy to contextualise interventions adequately

Religious literacy is key to developing capacities for context and faith-sensitive engagements with religion, and adequate religious literacy is a prerequisite for effective contextualisation of interventions. Building religious literacy involves understanding the basic tenets of religion, including the multiple interpretations and contentions. Religious literacy emphasises the context-specific nature of religious practices and demands a process of mutual engagement with religious actors. Such engagement relies not only on striving to understand the religious actors' self-understanding but also to recognise your understanding of yourself and your own biases. This must be brought into conversation with the VAWG objectives at hand in a specific cultural context, allowing for honest engagement with the diverse roles that religious actors can play in promoting or hindering VAWG (Moore, 2015a, 2015b).

Practitioners and policymakers need to be aware that religious understanding continually and dynamically evolves in a social setting, which requires, in turn, continued engagement and monitoring of religious moods, motivations and manifestations in religious communities. Religious literacy is essential for practitioners and policymakers to understand how religion plays out and interacts with culture in gendered ways, driving or countering VAWG over time and place. Therefore, engaging with religion to address VAWG requires building the religious literacy of practitioners to ensure VAWG interventions are tailored to respond to existing religious manifestations and contentions in religious communities. By developing religious literacy, practitioners are empowered to recognise and mitigate religious-related risks of VAWG, including (1) conceptual risks such as religious (mis)beliefs; (2) behavioural risks such as religious (mis)practices and (3) spiritual and emotional risks such as meanings of religious experiences, often leading to enduring VAWG and gendered harms.

Prioritising religious literacy also means moving beyond Abrahamic religions – Judaism, Christianity and Islam – to strengthen capacities to work with a variety of religions in the non-Abrahamic world. More engagement is needed with other and diverse religions, including indigenous and traditional religions, impacting millions of people worldwide. To date, there is a disproportionate volume of scholarship on VAWG and Abrahamic religions. Further research should expand our understanding of non-Abrahamic religions in relation to VAWG to thus enable religious engagement in wider and under-researched settings influenced by diverse religions.

Implication 6: Use a hybrid and pragmatic understanding of religion

Parts II and III explore the positive and adverse intersections of religion and VAWG; based on the conceptual framework we deployed to engage with the substance (*what religion is*) and functions (*what religion does*) of religion. Our empirical chapters indicate the importance of accounting for both the substantial and functional meanings of religion, for only by using such a hybrid understanding can the full spectrum of reach and influence of religion be captured. We encourage researchers, practitioners and policymakers to use a hybrid understanding of religion, combining the functional and substantial, as it allows engagement with the wide reach of religious influences as well as religious complexities, more effectively. Especially when it comes to understanding and addressing VAWG such a hybrid understanding of religion is important, as it enables an understanding of what religion does in shaping VAWG experiences, through allowing understanding of what religion is. For example, a woman's decades-long endurance of domestic violence can only be fully understood (and potentially addressed) in the light of her religious belief in eternal life and reward in the life hereafter. Religious constructs shaping the VAWG experience often draw on the transcendent beliefs in the invisible world, either supporting or undermining the survivors' well-being and providing or obscuring resources for VAWG mitigation and response. Therefore, expanding the conceptual understanding of religion in VAWG is of paramount importance to ensure lived experiences of religion in VAWG are understood and responded to adequately by research, policy and practice.

At the same time, a pragmatic understanding of religion is also important in the light of the diversity and complexity of religious expressions. A pragmatic approach enables us to deal with religion in lived experience sensibly and realistically, drawing on the subjective and practical meaning of religion in people's lives. As the theoretical definitions of religion may not adequately capture how religion is understood and lived in local communities, it is important to engage with religion according to how it is understood by those who adhere to it. A real-life understanding of religion should interest us the most in VAWG research, policy and practice, as it enables us to understand lived experiences of abuse.

Implication 7: Bridge the divide between secular actors and religious actors

Stronger and more diverse partnerships between religious actors and secular actors are needed in order to ensure that Sustainable Development Goal 5 becomes a reality. Forging such partnerships is crucial for knowledge and know-how exchange. Facilitating dialogue and collaboration between secular and religious actors should be based on shared principles of respect and trust to facilitate efficient exchange and learning from one another while sharing the objectives of ending VAWG and supporting survivors. Further research can be helpful in identifying how collaboration between secular and religious actors addressing VAWG can be facilitated and strengthened, for the scale of the VAWG pandemic requires developing new ways of working and collaborating with multisectoral partners.

Religion should not be a niche area of exploration for a few select VAWG researchers, practitioners and policymakers. Rather, it should be recognised by all as part of the VAWG landscape. In this regard, it is important for the intersection between religion and VAWG to be more prominent on the VAWG research agenda so as to ensure the development of knowledge and evidence that can guide practitioners and policymakers in engaging with the religion and VAWG appropriately. To enable such research, there is a great need for methodologies and tools that are capable of embracing the complexity of religion. In developing these, researchers and practitioners need to work together to develop and test innovative approaches that can facilitate a better understanding of the functions and impacts of religion at the local level.

References

Moore, D.L. (2015a). *Our method*. Viewed from https://rlp.hds.harvard. edu/files/hds-rlp/files/rlp_method_2015.pdf [Date accessed: April 5, 2022].

Moore, D.L. (2015b). "Diminishing religious literacy: Methodological assumptions and analytical frameworks for promoting the public understanding of religion", in A. Dinham and M. Francis (eds.), *Religious literacy in policy and practice*. Bristol: Policy Press, 27–38.

Ter Haar, G. (2011). "Religion and development: Introducing a new debate", in G. Ter Haar (ed.), *Religion and development: Ways of transforming the world*. London: Hurst & Company, 3–25.

Williamson, J. and Robinson, M. (2006). "Psychosocial interventions, or integrated programming for wellbeing?", *Intervention*, 4(1): 4–25.

INDEX

Printed in the United States
by Baker & Taylor Publisher Services